FINICKY EATERS

P.J. and my daughter, Twink, had the same tastes in food. Spaghetti was something to be avoided, as were vegetables. It must have been a blow when Twink discovered that her pet couldn't be persuaded to share the vegetables she was commanded to eat. On a number of occasions the adults found mounds of string beans, cauliflower or carrots on the floor. Carrots, most of all. Twink always explained, with supreme innocence, that they must have dropped to the floor by accident, and never did she admit trying to palm them off on P.J.

P.J., MY FRIEND

NOEL B. GERSON

MANOR
BOOKS
INC.

A MANOR BOOK 1975

Manor Books Inc.
432 Park Avenue South
New York, New York 10016

Library of Congress Catalog Card Number: 69-20088

For
NOEL-ANNE
whom P.J. and I have always called "Twink,"
and for
JIM,
her husband

I

THE 98¢ CAT

When P.J. joined our family at the age of three months I told him I had paid $98 for him at the pet store on Lexington Avenue. Since he was only a kitten at the time, and therefore knew relatively little about matters of high finance, I am inclined to think he took my word.

Twink and I carefully maintained the fiction, and thereafter, whenever we mentioned the sum, were careful to wink at each other behind his back. More than fourteen years later, when the active, if not titular head of the family died, he still believed the story, or so we thought.

In fact, we were convinced that he never learned the truth, that I actually had paid 98¢, tax included, for him.

Just for the record, it was for our own sakes, not P.J.'s, that we concealed the facts of life from him. A natural aristocrat, he was "people," as six-year-old Twink remarked the week he came to live with us. Certainly he never deigned to think of himself as an ordinary, tiger-striped tabby, or in less polite language, an alley cat.

His values were lofty, and sometimes seemed arcane to lesser beings, including those of us who loved him and whom he loved. Dignity was all-important to him, even when he was in a playful mood. Since he *was* a cat, or so it sometimes seemed, he prized independence, both physical and spiritual. He was endowed with a reckless courage that was anything but catlike, and the sense of discretion he developed was, I am compelled to admit, a painfully acquired characteristic. Certainly there was nothing feline in the fierce loyalty he showed his intimates, and he expected a similar loyalty in return.

The story of P.J. and Twink really begins in 1950, when the heroine of the tale was two and one-half years old. Lee Barker, Doubleday's great editor and one of the most wonderful men I've ever been privileged to know, had just brought out my first novel, *Savage Gentleman*. It was successful, and encouraged my hope that I could some day devote my entire career to writing books; then I could give up the television and radio plays that, although they earned me a respectable income, forced me to live in New York City.

I have nothing against cities, having been born and reared in Chicago, but that was in a different era. The concrete jungle of the era after World War II, I believed, was no place to bring up a child. The belief had hardened into a conviction by the time Twink reached kindergarten.

She was a worldly, city child who often went to matinees, concerts and the ballet, somewhat less frequently to opera or the Radio City Music Hall. She enjoyed her classes at the "Y," where her insistently individualistic interpretations made her the despair of her modern dance teacher. She was at home on long airplane flights to the Caribbean, and on shorter jaunts to see Grandma and Grandpa in Chicago.

So many airline hostesses had taken her forward to watch the pilots at work that cockpits bored her, although she hadn't yet abandoned the thought of becoming a hostess herself when she grew up. She infinitely preferred trains—and still does. So do I, although the New Haven Railroad has tempered my enthusiasm. In any event, Twink loved the Twentieth Century Limited, and was sorry she wasn't a boy so she could become an Engineer Casey. All engineers were named Casey, after the hero of her favorite phonograph record, which she played daily, *ad nauseam.*

Skyscrapers held no terrors for her, and she loved the elevator that whisked her up to Daddy's 40th-floor office in a few seconds. But there were serious gaps in her development.

One of them, which was symptomatic, became painfully evident during a weekend visit to Ralph Ross, now of Scripps College and recently of the University of Minnesota, who was teaching that summer at Princeton. Soon after our arrival my wife and Twink went off for a canoe ride with Ralph, while I remained behind to lose, hopelessly, a debate with anthropologist Ashley Montague.

Ralph, a compassionate man as well as a distinguished educator, laughed wryly when the canoeists returned from their outing. "Twink was petrified," he reported. "The combination of water and grass and trees was too much for her. She was so desperately afraid that she talked a blue streak the whole time. A real city child who never stops verbalizing."

Obviously, the outdoor life of the city child is limited. Twink and her friend, Jeffrey Chasin, went to Central Park only when accompanied by a parent of one or the other. Her new friend, Annie Quintano, who lived in the building into which we had just moved, rarely went to the park. A very shy little girl, Annie didn't want to go out unless accompanied by her mother, whose mobility was limited by the impending birth of a new baby. To complicate matters, Jeffrey's family was building a house on Long Island, and Barbara Cantwell, another friend with whom Twink quarreled happily, was also moving out of the city.

At just this time it became even more difficult for Twink, living in a shrinking world, to spend her post-kindergarten afternoon hours playing at home. I had taken the plunge into the full-time world of writing books, and, abandoning television, occasional magazine articles and other writing, had given up my office.

My study, or workroom, was a small maid's cell in the new apartment. Located off the kitchen and soon overflowing with bookshelves, it was cramped and, I quickly discovered, far from soundproof. Twink immediately felt the repercussions.

Under ideal circumstances the children of an author who works at home appreciate the value of silence, and react accordingly. Ha. Even in my present study, which is a separate building situated behind our house, my younger children, Michele, Margot and Paul, know there will be instant, perhaps violent, repercussions if they make too much noise and disturb me at work. So they use the swing at the bottom of the hill, wade in the brook or play with their friends in the yard *only* when the Ogre isn't locked behind his closed door.

Twink, an only child living in a Manhattan apartment, led a far more severely restricted existence. She couldn't watch TV while I was working, as I could hear the set blaring. She could entertain Annie or other friends behind the closed door of her own room, but it is cruelly confining when small children play for an extended period in such limited space. Unfortunately, there was little choice; shouts, screams and giggles of little people emanating from the living room, dining room or other portions of the apartment distracted the man at the typewriter, who sometimes struggled for long periods before words began to flow again.

The obvious solution was a move to the suburbs or beyond, but I was not yet prepared, financially and otherwise, to leap into the relatively open spaces. The prospect of living within commuting distance of the city did not attract me then, any more than it does now. I had seen too many friends burdened by the mores of suburbia and exurbia, and had no desire to be shackled by a hard-drinking, heavy-spending social life. If and when I left New York City, I wanted to be far enough away to live the kind of life I deemed appropriate for my daughter, yet remain within striking distance of the city.

I was gambling by putting all of my words into books, and at the back of my mind was the comfortable realization that, if necessary, I could grind out plays for television again, provided I continued to live close enough to the market place and maintained what the advertising agency boys call "contacts." So, for another couple of years, we were forced to maintain our imperfect existence as cliff dwellers.

In all honesty, I was emotionally unprepared for a do-it-yourself existence as a modern country squire, too. Although I had lived for several brief periods in rented houses, I was still a city boy. There were vast differences between my own upbringing on Chicago's South Side, where there were open fields and a lakefront as yet uncontaminated by beaches, where children could play unsupervised, and Manhattan tower existence, where youngsters—particularly the offspring of authors—found it almost impossible to breathe freely.

The urgency of the immediate problem was underscored by a number of little incidents, none of which was important but, when added to the sum of all the others, became significant. One warm summer Saturday we drove to a Long Island beach club with some friends, their daughter, who was a year older than Twink, and their handsome German shepherd dog. Twink was cowed by the animal, who was as friendly as he was regal, and shrank from him in the confines of the automobile.

A week or two later we went up to Westport to visit old friends, Florence and Hal James. Hal, then chained to television, which he disliked as ephemeral and trifling, and subsequently able to earn his lifelong dream of becoming a theatrical producer when he presented the enormously successful *Man of La Mancha,* is a genial man with an instinctive understanding of children. The three James youngsters were away at summer camp, or wherever, and Hal, feeling sorry for Twink, repeatedly urged her to go out into the yard to play. She demurred, electing instead to remain with the grownups, so he and I finally went out into the yard with her.

She moved cautiously, inching a few steps in one direction, then another, and becoming rooted to a spot from which she refused to move. Her odd behavior made no sense, and when she could not or would not offer an explanation, I became annoyed.

But Hal gave me no chance to thunder at her. "You know," he said, raising a hand to silence me, "I think she's afraid of walking in deep grass."

He was right, and not until we mowed the lawn for Twink's benefit did she consent to play outdoors. Something had to be done, but I didn't know how to solve the dilemma.

Two straws blown by the winds of autumn that year pointed the way. One Sunday, when we were strolling homeward up Park Avenue after dining out, an inoffensive cat appeared on the sidewalk in front of us. Twink screamed, darted behind me and, clutching my legs, refused to budge until the cat moved on.

In vain I reminded her of Blackie, a cat which had "come with the house" we had rented in the hills above Kingston, Jamaica, when she had been several years younger. She couldn't remember Blackie, and in all justice I couldn't blame her. Blackie rarely came indoors,

17

appeared only at mealtimes to be fed by the cook and spent most of her days in the open field behind the house, catching mice and eating lizards, which disagreed with her digestion.

But it became apparent on Halloween that Blackie had left an imprint on Twink. City children go trick-or-treating within the confines of their apartment houses, and there was great excitement as Twink and Annie made their plans for the event. Twink insisted on "dressing in a kitty costume," and at last the obvious, waved under parental noses for so long, became clear.

Twink needed a pet of her own, preferably a cat. Her pediatrician heartily endorsed the idea, and so did Angie, the genial nursemaid who picked her up at kindergarten every day at noon and looked after her until bedtime.

I am forced to admit I was less than overjoyed. I was a dog lover who knew nothing about cats, and in my own boyhood had owned a black chow I still recalled with nostalgic pleasure. On the other hand, I knew the penalty of keeping a dog in a city apartment: someone would have to walk the animal several times daily, and I'd be elected. So, although I was still dubious, a cat seemed to be the lesser evil.

Late the next afternoon, my day's stint on the typewriter completed, I carried my misgivings with me to a pet store several blocks from our apartment house, totally unaware of the transformation that would take place in my own life as well as in Twink's. The lights were still burning, and a man was sitting at a desk in the rear of the shop, muttering to himself as he added figures in a ledger.

If I were writing fiction I'd present the proprietor of the pet store as a jolly fellow who loved all animals, and in justice to the man it may be that his day had been rough and unprofitable. My request certainly did nothing to improve his disposition.

"Do you have any kittens for sale?"

He jerked a thumb in the direction of a sawdust-coated bin at the rear of the store. "If that's what you want to call 'em."

I went to the bin and peered uncertainly at several small, tiger-striped gray animals, all of them sleeping. All but one continued to sleep.

The kitten curled up at the rear of the bin opened his green eyes, raised his pointed ears and subjected me to a cool, thorough inspection.

I later claimed I was amused, and therefore made no move. To be honest, I believe I was stunned by the animal's calm audacity.

He effortlessly stood, stretching his hind legs and yawning, and then came toward me for a closer examination. A small brown nose sniffed at my hand in what I mistakenly thought a canine rather than a feline reaction, and before I knew what was happening, a firm little creature landed on my shoulder.

In my ignorance of cats I tried to remove him by tugging at him instead of moving him forward, so that his claws cut through the thick fabric of my topcoat.

The proprietor rescued me. "Is this the one you want?"

"If it's a male." Someone had told us, for reasons that have become irrelevant as well as silly, that males were preferable to females.

A brief examination by the proprietor indicated that the kitten was qualified to join our household.

"How much do you want for him?" I asked.

The man thought for a moment, no longer. "You can have him for 98¢."

As I write these words it occurs to me, for the first time, that P.J. heard our conversation, and no matter what we later told him, knew the truth all along. Provided he was listening.

I bought several cans of cat food and a bag of kitty litter, too, and the owner of the shop rummaged in what looked like a trash pile until he found a small, dilapidated cardboard box. He punched several airholes in it, dumped the kitten inside and secured the lid with a small length of flimsy twine.

I started home, the cat food and kitty litter in a large paper bag in one hand, the box under my other arm.

Ordinarily twilight is my favorite time of day in the city. The grime becomes only semi-visible, the anxieties on the faces of pedestrians are softened, and lights burning behind the windows of tall buildings recapture for me the enchantment of New York I had known in childhood visits to the city, when I had promised myself I would live there some day.

That evening, however, I endured sheer torture. The kitten hated the confinement of the dark box, a loathing he would continue to feel when placed in a cat cage at one time or another throughout his life. He howled in frustrated rage, his voice louder than I had imagined possible, and my embarrassment was excruciating when passersby, pouring out of the Lexington Avenue and 86th Street subway station paused in their homeward rush to gape at me.

But the kitten's protests were the least of my troubles. It began to dawn on me that I had acquired no ordinary pet when the top of the box was pushed upward, the twine already broken, and a small paw appeared in the opening. Afraid the animal would escape, I dumped the brown paper bag on the sidewalk, clamped down the lid of the box and tried in vain to secure it. I have no idea how many times I was forced to halt, and I felt certain, as I headed toward Park Avenue, that the kitten, for whom I already felt responsible, would leap out and vanish in the streets.

Somehow we reached the apartment building, where the doorman raised a polite eyebrow. The elevator was filled when I entered it, and everyone, including my next-door neighbor, Jim Yuill, a talented painter and advertising agency art director, was laughing by the time we reached my stop, the ninth floor. I was bathed in sweat and silently cursing.

Twink had just finished her evening meal and reluctantly interrupted the highlight of her day, the *Howdy Doody* TV program, to come into the front hall in response to my shout that she present herself at once.

I placed the box on the floor and, simultaneously, the kitten popped out.

Twink's fear of animals was forgotten as, in silent ecstasy, she dropped to her knees and held out her arms.

The kitten, not hesitating an instant, went to her. It is the only time in my life I have ever been privileged to witness a mutual declaration of love at first sight, a love that would endure for almost a decade and a half until, after Twink had raced home from college for twenty-four hours just before her mid-term exams to see a failing P.J., I had to call her at school the next day to tell her the end had come.

But now, as the little girl carried her kitten into the living room and, still silent, sat down to cradle him in her arms as he "rumbled like a motorboat," the bright years and the aching void that followed it were still ahead. In an adjoining room the forgotten television set blared; it was the only time in Twink's young life that she allowed anything to prevent her from watching *Howdy Doody*.

At last the kitten stirred, and Twink took him on a tour of the apartment, explaining the function of each room to him. Suddenly she stopped. "Which is going to be his bathroom?" she wanted to know.

My wife explained the purpose of the kitty litter, which

she had already placed in a pan on the floor of what, in earlier, more grandiose times, had been the butler's pantry of the apartment.

The kitten leaped to the floor, and a delighted Twink followed him into the kitchen which he had not yet seen. "He's hungry," she announced.

We allowed her to pour a bowl of milk for him, and no one minded when she spilled some on the floor. The kitten drank some milk, but spurned the cat food that Twink put down for him. Instead he leaped onto the kitchen counter, and only my wife's agility saved the raw, chopped steak that had been taken out of the freezer to defrost before being cooked for the adults' dinner.

"Can't you see he wants hamburger?" Twink demanded.

The grownups looked at each other, silently agreed to open a can of corned beef hash and let Twink give the kitten the hamburger. He ate carefully, daintily, like a true gentleman, and then went straight to the kitty litter pan, which he had not yet been shown. It was an impressive performance.

Some time later, after a bounding kitten and a wildly excited child had exhausted themselves chasing through the apartment, the animal fell asleep on the little girl's lap, and Twink made an important announcement. "His name," she said, "is Prince."

I flinched, thinking that only Rover would have been a worse name, but managed to keep silent. I like to think I was sufficiently mature to smile in approval. Perhaps I did. Weakly.

Eventually a drooping child was persuaded to go to bed. It had grown too late for her bath, and she was so tired she had to be undressed and clad in her pajamas. But she had enough strength to murmur, as she hugged the kitten, "Good night, sweet Prince."

The adults consoled each other with the thought that not too many kittens were named Prince Hamlet.

I brooded through the meal of corned beef hash, however. Something had to be done about the kitten's name. That's all there was to it.

I was interrupted by noises from Twink's room, and found a sleepy child and equally sleepy kitten romping on her bed. Calling a stern halt to the game, I told her as I placed the animal outside the covers and tucked her in bed, "He has a middle name. It's Julius."

She was too sleepy to argue.

I've often been asked how I happened to give the kitten his middle name, and I'm afraid I don't know. It may be that the name was in my mind because I was doing a novel on Caesar and Cleopatra that, in due time, Doubleday published as *That Egyptian Woman*. On the other hand, it may be because the name somehow fitted.

Whatever the reasons, the new arrival's full name was Prince Julius Hamlet, but he was addressed formally only when being chastised. By the next day all of us started calling him P.J., and P.J. he remained. His auxiliary pet names came into being one by one, gradually, but I can't jump ahead of the sequence of events.

It's enough, I think, to conclude this chapter with the realization that came to me later that evening: something extraordinary had happened. I knew it when I looked in at a sleeping Twink and found a sleeping P.J. curled up beside her, his head on the pillow, her hand on his soft fur. I knew so little about cats that I disapproved of an animal sleeping so close to a child, but I didn't have the heart to move P.J. elsewhere.

Even then I sensed that Twink and P.J. had already formed a very special relationship.

II

THE BEST FRIENDS

The morning after P.J.'s arrival, I emerged from my bedroom to find a spectacle awaiting me in the dining room. I've claimed for many years that I'm a zombie until I've had a large mug of coffee, but this was one morning when the sight that greeted me had an immediate effect. I needed no coffee to awaken me.

A small child and a smaller kitten were sharing an intimate breakfast. Twink, who must have arisen before dawn, had prepared the meal herself, knocking only a few boxes and jars from a shelf to get a box of crispy, crunchy cereal, and spilling only small quantities of milk.

The cereal and milk had been poured into a very large soup bowl, which could accommodate two. P.J. sat on the dining-room table, happily lapping milk and stray bits of cereal, and Twink, who ordinarily loathed cold cereal, was spooning her breakfast with unaccustomed serenity.

The fastidious adult intervened: the kitten was deposited on the floor, and the child received a lecture on sanitation.

Twink was heartbroken, and wept.

P.J., the pragmatist, jumped onto her chair with effortless grace and rubbed against her, purring, as he comforted her. Occasionally, when he thought I wasn't looking or was otherwise occupied, he craned his neck and imbibed a little more milk.

My speech was pungent and direct, and I concluded by saying, "Animals and people don't eat from the same dish."

Twink was outraged. "P.J. isn't an animal! He's a people!"

I was unable to disabuse her of the notion, so P.J. became people. Fortunately, Twink accepted my dictum that I would get rid of him if she fed him from her own plate.

Peace and reasonable sanitation restored, I went off for my coffee, returning to find P.J. helping himself from the cereal bowl, now on the floor, while Twink consoled herself with a doughnut, which she despised.

Before I could launch into a dissertation on nutrition, Twink created a diversion. "I'm your little girl," she said, "and you're my daddy. What are P.J. and I? I could pretend I'm his mummy and he's my little boy, but we aren't *really*. What are we?"

I gulped some coffee, lighted a cigarette, coughed and groped for an answer.

She became a trifle scornful. "And you aren't his daddy!"

"No," I muttered. "I'm his friend."

Twink digested this information. "Is he your friend?"

"Of course." The problem, it appeared, wasn't as difficult as I had thought.

Again she was silent, and there was no sound in the room but that of the hungry kitten lapping up milk. "But I'm *more* than just his friend," she announced at last.

I had no intention of making an issue of the point.

"And he's more than just my friend!" The child's tone was strident, but behind it was a hint of the firmness she would develop in the years ahead.

"You betcha," I said, heartily sick of the subject and wanting to collapse somewhere with my coffee.

"I know!" Twink was triumphant. "We're *best* friends!"

And so they were, in a relationship that put Damon and Pythias to shame.

The Best Friends were inseparable. Twink wept when forced to go off to kindergarten without her boon companion. P.J. compounded the situation by dashing out of the apartment door after her and accompanying her to the elevator. Luckily, there were only four apartments on our floor, so it was relatively easy to catch him and take him inside again. By "relatively easy," I mean that one or two adults might be able to get their hands on him after a five- to ten-minute chase.

From the first, Twink considered it her prerogative to

prepare P.J.'s meals, and felt insulted when we sometimes told her his dishes required more scrubbing. He invariably slept with her, too, sometimes curling up beside her, sometimes sprawling across her. When locked out of her room, he sat beside the closed door, yowling until she awakened and let him in. Even the strictest parent surrenders after being treated to this sort of conspiracy every night.

P.J. established an immediate rapport with Twink's friends. He liked Annie, he enjoyed Barbara's company and he tolerated Jeff, difficult though it may have been for him to endure the manhandling of a small boy. I've always marveled at the sensitivity of cats and dogs in this respect. I've known any number who make no protest, submitting with good grace when little children maul them, yet have seen these same animals bite, snarl and claw when subjected to far less severe physical treatment by an adult.

I have no doubt that P.J. knew children couldn't help being a bit rough, and he allowed them liberties that he permitted no older person. For many years after he and I made our peace he would nip at me if he thought I was treating him with less than the dignity he deserved. But Twink and her friends could tumble him from a lap, wrestle with him or grasp him with grubby hands, and his only reaction would be a quiet purr of happiness.

That sound, commonly identified as a purr, came under close scrutiny after P.J. had spent a few days in the family. Twink didn't like the word, so I tried to help her find another. She told me I was silly when I suggested he sounded like an airplane engine or a locomotive. I made several other attempts, but gave up when they were rejected.

"You tell me what he sounds like," I said, challenging her.

Twink's calm was monumental. "He rumbles, doesn't he?"

I was forced to agree that he rumbled.

"Well," she said with the irrefutable logic of a six-year-old, "he rumbles just exactly like a motorboat!"

That's what he did for the rest of his life, and all of our other, additional cats have rumbled like motorboats, too. In fact, to this day Twink can't hear a motorboat without being reminded of P.J.'s rumble.

The volume of sound that kitten could achieve was amazing. I emerged from my study late one afternoon, groggy after a long session with Caesar and Cleopatra, and heard but could not see the motorboat. The noise filled the dining room, so I was able to trace it to its source, and discovered the Best Friends sprawling together under the dining-room table. Twink was whispering, and P.J. was agreeing by purring loudly.

Naturally I was curious.

"We're playing Sphinx," Twink explained.

A book on the ancient world that my sister had given her for her birthday had created an impression that has lasted to the present day. It was the initial spark that caused her, many years later, to elect anthropology as her college major. I had seen her staring at a photograph of the Great Sphinx of Giza, and knew she had been daydreaming, but had been unable to learn what was going through her mind. I made another attempt now.

"How do you play Sphinx?"

"Oh, we just do it." She retreated into the child's secret world.

P.J. glared at me, too, but continued to rumble.

"Is P.J. the Sphinx?"

Twink giggled, turned back to her pet and whispered to him again. Both of them were very happy.

So I went my own way and took solace in my stiff, pre-dinner bourbon-on-the-rocks.

It is small wonder that P.J. scorned cat food, and would eat it only when nothing else was available. Twink insisted on sharing her meals with him. No threats, scoldings or punishments could persuade her to abandon the practice. And she turned a deaf ear when told he had his own plate and milk dish in the butler's pantry.

"He gets lonely there, eating all by himself," she said. "He wants to eat with me."

The adults continued the struggle for years, but in vain. When Twink sat down to a meal, P.J. materialized and quietly sat beside her in the certain knowledge he would be fed a steady stream of tidbits. I'm forced to admit that his table manners were impeccable. After his first breakfast in the house he remembered that his place was on the floor, not on the table, and he was tempted to forget his manners only when we dined on roast turkey.

Even then he was a gentleman. Very delicately he raised his front paws to the lap of his Best Friend, or to that of an ordinary Friend. If ignored, he meeowed once, softly. If instructed to remove himself elsewhere, he dropped to the floor again. Usually the affront of a direct rebuff was too great to be tolerated, and he stalked away from the table, making a grand exit from the dining room.

Turkey was turkey, of course, so he soon returned to repeat the gestures.

Cats are the most persistent of creatures, as I've learned through the years. And P.J. was the most persistent of cats. Eventually he was given his scraps of turkey, or whatever. And the adults were given a tongue-lashing if something wasn't saved for his plate. In fact, Twink consistently refused to finish her own meal unless given assurances that there was enough for P.J., too.

The Best Friends had similar tastes in food. Hamburger was their favorite, and they much preferred it to steak, which, however, they would consent to eat. They loved chicken, and Twink made a ritual of breaking the wishbone, giving P.J. his part to hold in his teeth. They loved swordfish and tunafish, and did their elders a favor by eating salmon, but under no circumstances would touch sea bass or fresh mackerel. P.J., unlike his Best Friend, enjoyed a snack of canned mackerel. They were willing to tolerate lamb and veal, found bacon a joy at weekend family breakfasts, but had no use for ham.

They found cold cereals palatable, but Twink was in her teens before she liked oatmeal. Even then she ate it somewhat guiltily, knowing that P.J. didn't share her taste. Chocolate cake sent them on their separate ways, too, but Twink didn't mind, readily eating what she called "P.J.'s piece" as well as her own.

Spaghetti was something to be avoided, as were vegetables. It must have been a blow when Twink discovered that her pet couldn't be persuaded to share the vegetables she was commanded to eat. On a number of occasions the adults found mounds of string beans, cauliflower or carrots on the floor. Carrots, most of all. Twink always explained, with supreme innocence, that they must have dropped to the floor by accident, and never did she admit trying to palm them off on P.J.

One night her loathing for carrots created domestic havoc. My wife and I were dressing to go out for the evening, and Angie was busy in the kitchen, so Twink and P.J. sat by themselves in the dining room, eating meat and potatoes, and trying to avoid carrots. As we later pieced together the incident, Twink went off to the bathroom, always a legitimate excuse for leaving the table.

By the time we learned what was happening, it was too late. Catastrophe had struck. Water was gushing out of the toilet in Twink's bathroom, pouring through her bedroom into the corridor beyond it, soaking the carpet and threatening to transform the entire floor of the apartment into an indoor lake.

The child stood near the geyser, alternately laughing and weeping. P.J., who had been inundated by the initial overflow after accompanying his Best Friend to the bathroom, was an outraged, soaked kitten. He flew about the apartment, leaping onto bookshelves, tables and chairs, complaining in a loud, bitter tone as he left everything he touched dripping in his wake.

I hurried into the bathroom to stem the flow, while my wife, aware of my ineptitude in such matters, summoned the building superintendent. The "supers" of Manhattan apartment buildings are necessarily jacks-of-all-trades, able to cope with any domestic crisis, and John was no exception. The flow was halted, and, while my wife and I started to remove the waterlogged carpets, John took apart the pipes to see what had clogged the toilet.

What he found was a large mass of sliced carrots.

P.J. meeowed piteously, sympathizing with all his heart as he watched his Best Friend being spanked.

It was no trick at all to prevent P.J. from dashing out the back door of the apartment. When someone rang the back-door buzzer, the kitten was moved from the room, the swinging door that led to the butler's pantry was closed, and escape for the playful animal was impossible.

The front door posed another, far more serious problem. There were arches but no doors that shut off the large entrance foyer from the living room and dining room, and often the doors of bedrooms that opened onto the main corridor beyond the living room were open, too.

P.J. quickly learned that the front door made a sound of its own when opened, and he loved to make a wild, scampering dash into the corridor. He considered it a great game, running with all his might, a gray streak with his ears flattened close to his head and his tail extended straight behind him. He was encouraged by his Best Friend, who shrieked in delight, knowing the pastime was forbidden and that he was succeeding in defying Authority.

He was so agile and fast that it was almost impossible to catch him before he reached the outer corridor. Even when two or more adults stood guard, P.J. had the advantage of surprise, and utilized his tactics with the cunning of Alexander the Great maneuvering his small force on the ponderous flanks of the Persian host. Often we had no way of guessing P.J.'s vantage point. He might be hiding under a chair or table, on the shelf of a bookcase or in any one of a score of other hideouts. When the front door opened, the gray streak appeared out of nowhere and reached the restricted zone.

There was nothing in the corridor but the doors to the other apartments, which were almost always closed, the door leading to the back stairs, which was stuck and couldn't be opened by anyone except John, the superintendent—and the elevator door. It, magically, opened from time to time, and I imagine that P.J., like Twink, always wondered who might be inside the elevator.

He made many, determined efforts to find out, and sometimes succeeded. Whenever I saw him disappear into the elevator, I shouted as I chased after him. Always some startled passenger pushed a button to keep the door open. Always P.J. was busily becoming acquainted with his new-found friends, regardless of whether they liked cats. And always I was forced to retrieve him, red-faced and stammering my apologies.

New Yorkers are said to be cold and distant, but I urge readers in other parts of the country not to believe the canard. Not once did I encounter an irate or indifferent elevator passenger. Without exception these good men and women were kind, patient, helpful—and amused. Frequently they offered to take the kitten, and just as frequently I was eager to accept, but, for Twink's sake, forced myself to refrain.

P.J. made no attempt to conceal his irritation when his elevator-hopping fun was spoiled. He informed me in a loud, surprisingly deep voice that I was an old crab, a spoilsport and a bully. He also made frantic attempts to break away from me, efforts which taught me very early in our relationship how to hold and carry a kitten. Later, after he became adult, no one had the strength and dexterity to hold or carry him when he decided to move around under his own cat-power. Even when very small he showed signs of that fierce independence, and it was a major feat to carry three or four pounds of squirming, indignant kitten a dozen or so steps into the apartment.

Occasionally, when we and our neighbors happened to open our front doors simultaneously, P.J. went for a social call, ignoring the unwritten law that a New Yorker's home is inviolate, and that one pays a visit only when invited. These forays were even more embarrassing than his attempts to hitchhike an elevator ride.

P.J.'s curiosity was even greater than that of his proverbial progenitors, and he made a thorough inspection of every room in a strange apartment. Sometimes he made his investigation warily, ready to spring aside and duck under a bed or chair if someone tried to scoop him up. But just as often he played the game that Twink called "race horse." Simple in both concept and execution, it consisted of one small animal running at top speed through an apartment, sightseeing on the run and defying anyone to catch him.

These jaunts into the apartments of neighbors posed some perplexing problems that strained etiquette to the breaking point. Did I offer to follow the kitten through the strange precincts, shattering the privacy of unwilling hosts? Or did I indicate, delicately, that I would wait at the front door while they exercised their own ingenuity in finding ways to shoo him toward me?

I never did resolve the question to anyone's satisfaction. One of our neighbors was a dowager from Boston whose equally stuffy daughter and son-in-law spent part of each week with her. We were on the barest of nodding terms, and nothing could have persuaded me to cross their threshold. P.J. didn't share my inhibitions, however, and I was horrified when, early one morning, as I was going downstairs for the day's mail, he disappeared into the inner recesses of their austere sanctum.

The dowager, dressed for a matinee of the Boston symphony in spite of the early hour, coolly informed me she would bring the kitten to me, and asked me to wait. I smoked several cigarettes, listened in vain for an indication of what might be happening and peered through the foyer into the living room, but did not dare follow.

After an interminable wait, the old lady reappeared, cradling a contented P.J. in her arms. "See to it," she informed me severely, "that he's fed Canadian bacon from time to time. He's very partial to it, and to light cream."

P.J. was too full and sleepy to protest when I took him home. Twink was delighted when she heard of his adventure, and I suspect that she encouraged similar jaunts.

The high point—or nadir—of his visits to neighbors occurred when he was seven months old, sufficiently mature, in my firm opinion, to have known better.

The social life in our apartment house was unusual, it being an old custom for New Yorkers to be on no more than vaguely polite speaking terms. But we lived in a building brimming with kindred spirits, and at least two or three Fridays of each month a group of five or six couples gathered informally for cocktails. The wives worked out a now-it's-our-turn round-robin schedule, but the husbands had far more important matters on their minds. They played a game—in deadly earnest—and I soon found myself a grim and determined player.

The object of the game was to steal one's cocktail glass.

One was permitted to steal two glasses, but that was the limit. There were other, rigid rules. The hostess was not allowed to give the alarm if she spotted a guest with a glass hidden beneath his jacket. Only the host was permitted to apprehend a culprit, and when he did, of course, the glass was surrendered. The basic rule of the game was very strict: the couple giving a cocktail party were required to use expensive glassware. Any husband and wife who tried to use fifty-cent glasses would have been cheating, and undoubtedly would have been ostracized.

After spending a number of months on the building's cocktail circuit, one could see one's own glassware in everyone else's apartment, and could accept the situation with equanimity. Everyone had everyone else's glasses, and it wasn't considered sporting to steal back one's own.

The wives, to be sure, held the game in low esteem and condemned their husbands as adolescents. What they failed to realize was that a man had no real choice. Some of my best cocktail glasses had vanished after I'd been the host at two parties, and I had to recoup my losses. Necessity made me fairly adept at the game, but I wasn't in a class with Ed English, a distinguished Wall Street stockbroker who could have earned a splendid living as a kleptomaniac.

The champion, however, was Jim Yuill, my next-door neighbor. His artist's hands were very quick and nimble, and he had acquired the building's most impressive collection of glassware. Ordinarily I'd have had no chance to even the score, but a rare opportunity presented itself. Jim and his lovely wife, Peggy, a talented Seventh Avenue dress designer, were giving a large party with a guest list that extended beyond the limits of the group in the building. According to the unwritten rules of the game, one was allowed to steal four glasses from such an affair. Jim had a new set of highball glasses, each with a different sailing ship hand-painted on it, and I was thirsting for retaliation.

Angie was off duty for the weekend, so we hired a student nurse from a nearby hospital as a baby-sitter, and my wife and I went off to the party. This consisted of going out our front door and in the Yuill front door, which literally adjoined it.

Most large cocktail parties are dull, but this affair was an exception. There were enough people from the world of publishing, art, clothes designing, the theatre and the professions to make it sparkle. In spite of the usual big-party crush, the atmosphere was just right, and everyone was having a good time. I kept a firm grip on a hand-painted glass, and relaxed.

Then, suddenly, the atmosphere changed. One tiger-striped kitten whipped through the apartment, followed by one six-year-old girl clad in pajamas, bathrobe and slippers. Together they snaked in and out through a maze of adult legs, almost upsetting several staid drinkers, causing various ladies to coo in admiration, and, in an instant, destroying the ambiance of what had been a first-rate party.

The disruption had been easy to achieve. Our baby-sitter had gone off to the inner recesses of our apartment to use the telephone at some length. Laughter and other noises could be heard through our living-room wall, so Twink and P.J. had decided to make an investigation and find out what caused the sounds. They accomplished this by opening our front door. The Yuill door was already open, thanks to the guests still arriving in a steady stream, so the child and her cat joined the party.

I gave chase as best I could, but I was operating under a severe handicap. Guests were crammed into the living room, library and dining room, and I could shoulder them aside only by using a subway rush-hour technique, which was not acceptable behavior at a party. So the young culprits from my house were able to stay at least a room's headstart from me.

I heard myself calling, "Twink! P.J.!" but knew I was wasting my voice. If they heard me, which I doubt, as they were the center of so much attention, they chose to pretend otherwise.

When I finally caught up, the little girl and her kitten were having a party of their own in the kitchen. Twink was eating deviled eggs, which she usually wouldn't touch, and drinking a glass of milk without chocolate flavoring, to which she would have objected at home. P.J. was feasting on a plate of chicken livers wrapped in bacon and oysters wrapped in ditto.

I made menacing sounds.

"Now, really," Peggy Yuill said, handing Twink a large, chocolate cookie.

"There's no need to reward them for this," I snarled.

Any number of guests who thought Twink and P.J. were "cute" or "adorable" came out to the kitchen to see them, making it impossible for me to remove them at once. While I waited, they continued to gorge, and when Twink announced that P.J. was thirsty, he was given a bowl of light cream.

I glowered, but was impotent.

39

It seemed like a very long time before I could take the party-crashers away.

"Everyone enjoyed them," Peggy said, gracious and sincere. "And there was no harm done."

She was wrong. With a child in one arm and a kitten in the other, my hands were full, so I couldn't steal any of Jim's hand-painted glasses. In fact, when I returned to the party after depositing Twink and P.J. at home, I had an opportunity to take no more than one of the glasses I coveted. I look at it, often, and reflect that a golden chance was spoiled for me.

Twink won't know until she reads these lines why the glass with the sailing ship painted on it is always called, "Daddy's very special glass."

III

GETTING TO KNOW YOU

Forced by circumstances beyond our separate or joint control to live under the same roof, P.J. and I coexisted under cold war conditions that frequently became warm. At best we were politely tolerant, at worst we became very rude.

He had no use for a grouch who knew nothing and cared less about the psyche of a kitten. He must have found it disconcerting when, trying to demonstrate his openhearted nature, he climbed onto the back of the old ogre's chair in mid-evening and wiped a bushy tail across the shiny object people called eyeglasses. He had no way of knowing he was hindering research on an author's next book, and unquestionably felt hurt when he was dumped, without ceremony, on the floor.

So it went all day and part of the night. He slept with Twink, of course, and regarded her bed as his. But it was his prerogative to roam the house at will during the night, or so he believed, and from time to time he felt the need to assure himself that all was right with the world in the master bedroom. Unhappily for me, something was wrong with the latch, and the door could be opened with a slight but firm push. P.J., who had a genius for finding out all there was to know about his surroundings, discovered this fact by the time he was four months old.

Thereafter, every night without fail, he paid me a nocturnal visit.

I'm a light sleeper, and when I'm awakened in the night, I often stay awake for long periods. I couldn't blame P.J. for this quirk, but I condemned him without reservation for making a bad situation worse. Had he climbed onto my bed without fuss, quietly made himself at home near the foot and settled down in silence, I might have been able to tolerate his visits.

But he insisted on making them a star-spangled production. He announced his arrival by chatting, speaking with a series of short, staccato meeows, repeated in a brisk, business-like fashion, sometimes conversational, sometimes preemptory.

Awakened, I had to recognize his greeting. Sometimes I tried to placate him with, "Hi." More often I demanded, "What the hell do you want?"

As he well knew, I realized he wanted companionship, but he disliked ambiguity in his relationships, and carefully spelled out the reasons for his presence. Still talking the proverbial blue streak, he marched up and down the length of my recumbent body, pausing occasionally to knead the bedclothes. Of all the cats I've since known, P.J. was the champion kneader, and, if left undisturbed, could entertain himself for hours by burrowing.

If he had confined himself to these activities, I might have tolerated his presence. But he played two tricks guaranteed to arouse me. The simpler of them was a basic game, in which he pounced on one of my feet—"prounced," as Twink called it—digging his claws through the blankets until he struck human flesh. Then, when I invariably tried to pull away, usually in my sleep, he pounced again, still more ferociously. He stubbornly refused to respond to scoldings, spankings or the ultimate punishment, that of being heaved off the bed.

His other form of torture was far more subtle. Obviously knowing I was unaccustomed to cats, he approached the head of the bed while I was sound asleep, then rubbed against my face until I became conscious of the sensation. Without fail I jerked into an upright position, arms flailing, wide awake, cursing. P.J., having accomplished his mission, moved out of my reach and immediately left the room, gloating in a series of quietly satisfied meeows.

Something had to be done, and one morning at three o'clock I did it. I spent at least a quarter of an hour stumbling around the dark apartment until I caught him. Then, bringing him back to the bedroom, I treated him in dog fashion. With one hand I placed him at the head of the bed, and with the other I spanked him. After I had repeated the process a few times he clawed me and escaped.

I assumed I'd have more trouble, and was in despair. I had already asked the building superintendent to fix the master bedroom door, but knew from experience that his professional pride wouldn't permit him to make such a minor repair until I repeated my request, endlessly, for three or four months. So I wondered, naturally, how I could connive to insure myself an uninterrupted night's sleep.

I had failed to rely on P.J.'s intelligence. For whatever his reason, perhaps the spanking, but more probably his sense of fair play, he decided my demand was reasonable. The following night, not in the least discouraged by the treatment he had received, he paid me his usual visit. Announcing his presence and kneading, he advanced up the bedclothes as far as my shoulders. Then he halted abruptly, curled up on the bed and dropped off to sleep.

For the rest of his long life, never once slipping into the habits of his kittenhood, P.J. observed my rule. Never once did he approach my face or move higher on my bed than my shoulders. He knew Twink welcomed him on her pillow, no matter what adults might think of the practice. But he made it his business to respect my idiosyncrasy, and became so considerate I no longer had the heart to throw him off the bed.

It occurred to me for the first time that he was a gentleman in alley cat's fur, and I began to suspect he was endowed with a sense of humor.

There may be some who would say I was growing fond of him, that he was teaching me to give up my prejudices against cats. That would be arrant nonsense. It's true that

I recognized certain sterling qualities in him, knowing that no creature is all bad. And I appreciated the deep relationship he and Twink had formed. But that didn't mean I liked the beast.

On the contrary, I found him a nuisance. I was very annoyed one evening, when returning to the living room, to discover that P.J. had made an impossible tangle of several balls of expensive yarn my wife was using to knit me a sweater I had long wanted. We spent hours, without success, trying to straighten the mess, and the yarn had to be thrown away. I never did get my sweater; the yarn was imported from Scotland, and the manufacturer had stopped making it. I glowered at P.J. behind Twink's back.

If a little girl disobeyed orders and fed her kitten at the table when no one was looking, it was difficult to stop her. But that didn't mean I had to spoil P.J. As I frequently told him, his plates were on the butler's pantry floor, mine were on the dining-room table. Each of us had his clearly assigned eating place.

P.J. could be very dense when it suited his purposes, ignoring orders he had no intention of obeying. No matter what I said, no matter how resolutely I paid no attention to him when he followed me to the dining-room table, there he was. As a rule he sat near me, his green-brown eyes limpid and reproachful, his brown nose twitching. One needed will power to resist his appeal, but I had to prove that no mere animal could master me, so I tried not looking at him.

He first developed his special voice for dining-room use. His meeow was very soft, very weak, and there was a pitiful, pleading note in it that David Garrick would have envied.

I found it impossible to resist glancing at P.J. when he gave me his special treatment.

At that point, knowing he was ahead, he nailed down his victory. His expression unchanged, he repeated the sad meeeow, silently.

Knowing when I was beaten, I capitulated and fed him scraps of meat.

By now I've had a number of cats who will take food direct from my hand, but P.J. was never one of them. He sniffed a tidbit, but refused to touch it until it was placed on a plate, a paper napkin, or, if it wasn't greasy, on the floor. Only when given roast turkey did his desire force him to break his own rule, and then he bared his teeth and took hold of the far end of the meat. He took great care, always to refrain from biting the hand that fed him.

When he enjoyed a sliver, he asked for more, speaking in his brisk, conversational voice. Only when it wasn't forthcoming after he had made several polite requests did he resort to the sad little tone that melted steel. For a very long time I could not let myself believe that he was intelligent enough to be manipulating me. And by the time I gained a genuine respect for his IQ, our habit patterns had been formed.

My weakness in feeding him at the table caused complications, of course. As a reasonable father I could not demand that Twink refrain from doing what she saw me do. But I drew the line when she started saving the best morsels of food for her pet.

"P.J. likes white meat better than dark meat," she told me one Sunday when we were eating chicken.

I was outraged and insisted she eat the white meat her-self, an order that reduced her to tears.

In the main she was an obedient and respectful child, but she did not hesitate to defy me when her concept of P.J.'s well-being was at stake. No matter how severely I lectured her or tried to tell her it was wrong to give the best food to an animal when other children were starving in many parts of the world, P.J. continued to be fed his white meat, or its equivalent when we had other food than chicken.

Eventually I discovered that Twink was right, as she usually was in matters concerning P.J.: he really did pre-fer white meat. Luckily, I like dark just as well, so I had no reason to feel guilty, no reason to tell myself I was making a sacrifice for an animal's sake.

Dr. Sidney S. Greenberg, my physician and friend, is one of the wisest, most compassionate men I know. A life-long student of both internal medicine and psychiatry, he combines them brilliantly in his eminently successful practice. I've learned over a period of many years not to dispute Sidney; by the time he finishes telling me why I've chosen to argue with him, he has destroyed my position. He is also endowed with the skepticism that appears to be a personality trait in every experienced medical practi-tioner, and this makes him all the more formidable.

So I should have known better than to open the subject one evening when dining at the Greenbergs. Sidney's wife, Jill, had a dog which he disliked, or claimed to dislike, and he had no interest in other people's pets. Knowing all this, I can't for the life of me understand why I launched into a monologue on P.J.'s remarkable qualities.

Sidney yawned, and Jill tried to change the subject.

Goaded, I threw the supreme challenge at my host. "Our cat—Twink's cat," I said, "can count."

Sidney's eyes, behind his thick, horn-rimmed glasses, became guarded. "I beg your pardon?"

"Count," I said. "You know. One, two, three, four, five."

The other guests at the table stared down at their plates in silence. It was well known to all of them that authors were lacking in balance, and I wouldn't be the first to crack under the strain of rewrites.

But Sidney was equal to the emergency. "Come and see me at the office tomorrow," he said gently. "Call my nurse for an appointment, and she'll find time for you, no matter how busy I am."

"I'm serious about this," I told him.

His expression became grave. "So am I."

"Look," I said. "I have not flipped. Honest to God. I know it sounds crazy, but my daughter's cat can count, and I'll prove it to you."

I felt supremely self-confident, with good cause.

P.J.'s ability to count—you know, one, two, three, four, five—was an outgrowth of a disapproving or negative sound that everyone in our household made to discourage him from scratching furniture or doing other things that were forbidden. The sound, made in the back of the throat, almost as though one were clearing it, is forced out sharply. I can best illustrate it on paper as: *Enh!*

Someone must have told me it was effective, as I can't imagine inventing it myself. I do know it works, and P.J. as well as all the other cats who have since become members of our family have responded to *enh*. Spoken sharply and loudly, repeated when necessary, it deters a cat from doing something he shouldn't.

It was Twink, of course, who discovered that P.J. could count. I have no idea how she had become aware of his rather extraordinary talent, but she informed me of it one evening, as I finished my day's work and found her playing with her kitten, as usual, in the dining room.

"You know what, Daddy?" Twink was very calm. "P.J. can count."

"Don't be silly," I said irritably. "My rewrites didn't jell at all today." My mind was still on *That Egyptian Woman* and the extensive revisions in the manuscript that Lee Barker had suggested. Eventually his critique proved to be right, as always, but that didn't make it any easier for me to perform drastic surgery on the book.

"He doesn't believe us, P.J.," Twink said. "Listen, Daddy. *Enh*."

"Don't say that," I told her. "Save it for when he's doing something bad, otherwise he won't pay any attention."

"Please be quiet, Daddy. We can't show you if you keep talking, can we, Peejus? *Enh*."

P.J. looked at her, then cast his most superior glance in my direction. "*Enh*," he said, bored.

Accidents can happen, and I laughed.

"Daddy, you're awful. *Enh, enh*."

"*Enh, enh*," P.J. said.

My rewrites were forgotten. "*Enh*," I said, my excitement mounting. "*Enh, enh*."

P.J. yawned, stretched out on the dining-room rug and remained silent.

Again he replied when Twink addressed him.

Again he remained silent when I tried.

P.J.'s refusal to cooperate with me was mildly exasperating but unimportant. I urged Twink to experiment, and he repeated five *enhs* willingly, but refused to run the count any higher.

Wanting witnesses, I hurriedly invited Jim and Peggy Yuill over for a drink. Twink and P.J. performed for them, and they were duly impressed.

During the next week the little girl and her pet repeated the experiment many times. I shared her conviction that her cat was people, not an animal, and in my exuberance I made my rash boast at the Greenbergs.

In due course Sidney and Jill came to dinner, arriving late because he'd been delayed by a patient. Twink was already in bed for the night, so I should have kept my mouth shut. P.J. had been consistent in his refusal to perform for me, but for some illogical reason I felt sure he would when the chips were down.

I told the whole story, brought P.J. into the room and placed him on the arm of my chair. "*Enh*," I said.

The kitten decided to chase his tail.

"*Enh, enh.*" I was becoming desperate.

P.J. caught his tail, then played the game again.

"An ounce or two of whiskey," Sidney said, "can help a man relax after he's been subjected to mounting tensions all day. Drink your bourbon."

"*Enh, enh,*" I said.

P.J. thought the moment appropriate to take himself elsewhere.

I held him with a grip of iron, placed him on my lap and kept him there.

Everyone else tactfully changed the subject.

I continued to mutter at P.J., glaring at him.

He returned my stony gaze, and it was obvious we had reached an ultimate impasse.

I relaxed my grip for an instant, and he squirmed away from me, jumped to the floor and crossed the room to the sofa on which Sidney was sitting.

Even the kindest of physicians could not resist the opportunity. "*Enh, enh, enh,*" Sidney said, laughing.

P.J.'s expression was angelic. "*Enh, enh, enh,*" he replied.

In all the years I've known Sidney, that was the only time I've ever seen him accept a second pre-dinner drink. He refused, however, to discuss the phenomenon of the counting cat, and my own mortification was so great that I was happy to drop the subject.

I think P.J. was at least a year old before I could persuade him to reply to an *enh*. Even then he wouldn't do it to show off, but confined himself to a practical occasion. "*Enh, enh, enh,*" I told him when he jumped from the floor to a high bookcase shelf, causing a vase to wobble perilously.

He made himself comfortable on the shelf, nudging the vase closer to the edge. "*Enh, enh, enh,*" he said contemptuously, not only telling me to go to hell but giving me directions.

The defiance P.J. demonstrated on that occasion set a lifelong pattern. For the rest of his days he invariably replied in kind when rebuked with an *enh*. Only when Twink chastised him did he accept the injunction in silence; he refused to accept the family equivalent of "no" from anyone else.

On occasion, however, he felt compelled to police himself. The most notable incident occurred many years later, after we had moved from New York to the farther reaches of rural Connecticut. In our old New England house is a large walk-in closet where most of my clothes are kept. The high shelves above my suits and coats always fascinated P.J., who felt challenged by heights.

Since he could reach those shelves only by climbing up my clothes, admission to the closet was strictly forbidden. The state of repair of a suit's fabric was not improved when an exceptionally energetic cat used it as a ladder. So P.J. was removed from the closet many times when he entered on my heels, and after months of training he appeared to accept the ruling.

There is no insulation in the closet, which makes it bitterly cold on a New England winter morning. In order to alleviate the chill I developed the habit of opening the closet door en route to the bathroom first thing in the morning, making it relatively comfortable for me to enter a short time later.

One memorable morning, as I left the bathroom after my shower, I heard P.J. talking to himself. "*Enh, enh, enh,*" he was saying repeatedly in a soft but firm tone.

I investigated, and found him sitting outside the open door of the closet. He was looking with longing at the deliciously high shelves only a quick scramble away, and every quivering line in his body expressed his yearning. But he did not budge. "*Enh, enh, enh,*" he said again, then stood and sadly forced himself to retreat from temptation.

P.J.'s love of heights gave me one of the worst scares of my life one day during the latter stages of his kittenhood, and the incident certainly did nothing to improve our mutual affection and understanding.

Our Manhattan apartment was located on the ninth floor of a solid stone building with wide window ledges that had been built prior to World War II. It was L-shaped, the interior lining two sides of a concrete-floored courtyard. At the inner end of the L's short side stood our dining room, and across from it, on the longer arm, were Twink's bathroom, bedroom and, beyond them, another room or two.

One warm afternoon, when we had opened most of the windows, I was disturbed at my work by hearing Twink's thrilled, ecstatic squeals, and went from my study to the dining room to discover what mischief was being perpetrated. I entered just in time to see P.J., perching on the stone ledge of a dining-room window, leap five feet to the ledge of Twink's bathroom.

Under the best of circumstances I would have been horrified. I've suffered from vertigo all my life, and become dizzy just looking down out of a ninth-story window. In my youth, trying to cure myself of what I considered a character weakness, I had doggedly climbed the American and Canadian Rockies, the Swiss and Austrian Alps. Sad to relate, these efforts did not improve my condition; in fact, honesty compels me to admit that on every one of the many occasions I went climbing, I was terrified. The memory of the nightmare I endured for three days and nights on a Swiss glacier still causes me to break into a cold sweat.

I was frozen when I saw P.J. jump. Cats, I had learned, were not as sure-footed as their propagandists claimed, and only recently I had heard of a pet who had died making a somewhat similar leap.

P.J. landed outside the bathroom window, which was closed, his leap a graceful and effortless exercise. But he immediately found himself in trouble. The edge on which he landed was far narrower than those outside our other windows, and was no more than three inches wide. He was uncomfortable on the cramped precipice, and decided not to stay there.

It was obvious as he stood, testing his footing, that he intended to leap back to the dining room. It was equally obvious that he lacked the space on the narrow ledge to gather himself sufficiently for such a jump. If he tried it, the reckless gesture would fail, and he would crash to the cement nine stories below.

Telling Twink not to speak or make any gestures to attract the kitten, I dashed to her bathroom, and, approaching the window, began to speak to P.J. in what I hoped was a tone that would attract his attention. I know my voice shook, and I'm sure I spouted gibberish.

The window stuck, and would not budge.

I was afraid to strike it with my fist, since the unpleasant sensation might speed P.J.'s determination to make his return leap. To this day I don't know how I finally managed to raise that window, but after an agony of suspense I did.

In the same gesture I caught hold of P.J., grasping him so tightly that I must have squeezed the breath out of him.

He thought I was harassing him without cause, and became very indignant, swearing at me in a rambling stream of garbled, undertone meeowing.

I immediately closed every window in the apartment, and they stayed closed all night, even though we sweltered. Early the next morning I had glass wind and dust plates of glass installed, and instructed everyone in the house not to open the windows more than a few inches. I was determined to prevent P.J. from making another excursion to a window ledge.

I won the battle, but he tried every window in the house during the following weeks. And how he despised me for my cunning. Every time he failed to reach the outside ledge he looked at me reproachfully, then blasted me in a monologue that was more hurt in tone than sullen.

I thought him ungrateful, and our relationship was cool.

"P.J.," Twink often said, "is a professional squinger."

A professional, of course, is the best in his field. To squinge: a verb, sometimes a noun, invented by Twink. It describes a facial mannerism common to many, but not all cats. The animal indicates pleasure and sometimes flirts by slowly blinking his eyes. Simultaneously he crinkles—or seems to crinkle—the corners of his eyes, and at the same time smiles, or seems to smile.

The cat indulges in the gesture only when contented and wanting to express his affection. Usually he squinges while being stroked. P.J. is the only cat I've ever known who squinged at someone across a room, while sitting or sprawling alone.

The squinge is one of the most powerful weapons in a cat's arsenal. It drains away the hostilities of those who dislike him, and warms the indifferent. Invariably, it caused Twink to hug him fiercely, and, when I wasn't looking, kiss him. It wasn't sanitary to kiss him, she had been told, but that was a silly grown-up rule to be ignored and circumvented whenever possible.

P.J., I must admit, was a truly professional squinger. He squinged at Twink many times daily, which caused her to start a new round of hugging and general love-making. He squinged at my wife. He squinged at Angie. He squinged at all of Twink's friends, being fond of children. He squinged at our friends and casual acquaintances, including those who ignored him. Often he squinged at John, the building superintendent, who made no secret of his active dislike of cats.

Not once, in the first months after P.J. joined our family, did he squinge at me.

He demonstrated lesser forms of affection, it is true.

Frequently he climbed onto my lap, usually when I was reading and didn't appreciate being disturbed. He spent at least part of each night sleeping on my bed. Often he rumbled like a motorboat when I stroked him. But he refused to squinge at me.

I tried, hard, to break him down. I learned to stroke him in his favorite places, between his eyes and beneath his chin. He obligingly rumbled, but would not squinge, as he did for others. I began to feel we would never achieve more than a second-class friendship.

The change came unexpectedly, under circumstances that, initially, drove us farther apart. I realize now that P.J.'s initiative, not mine, was responsible for the rapport we finally achieved.

Circumstances had decreed that he and I spend the better part of our days together. Twink went off to school every morning, a half-day when she was in kindergarten, and until midafternoon when she moved onward and upward to first grade. She was escorted to school by my wife, who then went off for her own day in the glamour-marts as a high-fashion model. Angie arrived each day at noon to give Twink her lunch when she was still in kindergarten, and thereafter arrived in the early afternoon.

So only P.J. and I were left in the apartment. I went to my study for my usual day at the typewriter, and P.J. had the rest of the place to himself. I saw him occasionally, sleeping on one bed or another, resting in a living-room chair or sitting on the inside of a window, wishing he could reach the outer ledge. Now and again he used his kitty litter pan in the butler's pantry, just outside my study, which forced me to close my door. I suppose he thought I was shutting him out.

His food plate and his milk and water bowls were in the butler's pantry, too, so he reappeared from time to time for snacks. But he came into the study only when he wanted to tell me his food dish was empty. Then he approached, stood beside me and meeowed until I came up through several layers and recognized his presence. As soon as he knew he had caught my attention he trotted off to his dish, repeating the process until the old idiot finally realized he was hungry and wanted more food.

Then, one rainy morning when he had been with us for about six or seven months, P.J. finally decided to investigate my tiny study. Until then he had paid no attention to it, perhaps because he disliked the odor of tobacco smoke.

He roamed around my desk, sniffing, until I had to put him down. He made a brief but critical editorial examination of the new book I was writing for Doubleday, *The Impostor*. He chewed, experimentally, on a few of the pencils I kept on my desk in an old mug. And he tested his skills jumping from one bookshelf to another, a game that always gave him great pleasure.

An author, as a general rule, will use any excuse to avoid writing, so I didn't mind P.J.'s intrusion. I spent the better part of a half-hour watching him, chatting with him, eating up valuable time. But my deadlines couldn't be avoided, and I knew it, so I finally told him to enjoy himself and started to work.

P.J. stayed on the top of a bookcase for a time, surveying his realm from the heights, but eventually he found the inactivity boring. I should have realized what was developing when he sat on the floor near me, looking up, but by that time I was immersed in my manuscript and had put him out of my mind.

The sound of the typewriter, the popping up and down of its keys and the movement of its carriage attracted his attention. Maybe he liked the sound of the bell that rings at the end of each line. Like so many former newspapermen I use a beat-up old typewriter that clacks and rattles, that makes loud, authoritative sounds as I pound it. I've tried electric typewriters, and can't abide them.

Well, P.J. liked what he heard, too, or I may be doing him an injustice. Perhaps he felt sorry for the creature and wanted to put it out of its misery. Whatever his motive, he made one of his effortless leaps from a sitting position and landed in the middle of the typewriter.

The tab key had been struck, and the carriage shot to the end of the row, ringing the bell. P.J.'s paws became caught in the keys, and the harder he struggled to free himself, the more he became enmeshed. He howled in righteous anger and, perhaps, a touch of fright, although I'd never known him to be afraid of anything.

I tried to extricate him, but he inadvertently clawed me, making it almost impossible for me to catch hold of him. We struggled for some moments, and our joint efforts at last set him free. P.J. raced out of the room, hell-bent for escape from the contraption that had snared him, and I surveyed the damage. The typewriter, miraculously, had escaped unharmed, but an almost-completed manuscript page was ripped and had to be copied, a waste of time and effort that annoyed me. And, I discovered, some deep scratches on my hands and wrists were bleeding.

As I went off to my bathroom to wash my hands and stem the flow of blood, I caught a glimpse of P.J. He saw me, too, and vanished beneath Twink's bed, where he remained for the better part of the day.

That night I laid down the law. "I will not tolerate interference with my work!" I roared. "If that damn cat comes near my typewriter again, I'll get rid of him."

Twink went off to bed in tears.

The next morning, a short time after I started work, P.J. appeared in my study.

"What do you want?" I demanded rudely.

He meeowed and rubbed against my leg.

"Never mind the mush stuff," I said. "Keep your dirty mitts off my typewriter."

P.J. rubbed his face against my shoe, then stretched out across my foot and purring, dropped off to sleep. He spent the entire morning there. And that afternoon, when I returned from a business lunch date, he again accompanied me to my study. There he stayed until Twink came home from school, his behavior impeccable, his manners perfect.

When he reached the door he paused, then turned for a moment and squinged at me.

That day saw the beginning of a new routine. For the better part of the next year and a half, while we continued to live in the Manhattan apartment, P.J. was my constant daily companion. He spent both mornings and afternoons in my study with me while I worked, rarely venturing more than an arm's length from me, never interfering, never climbing on furniture, bookcases or, Heaven forfend, my typewriter.

I couldn't aspire to the status of a Best Friend. That would have been presumptuous. But P.J. and I were Friends at last, real Friends.

IV

THE GREEN-EYED MONSTER

As P.J. matured we gradually realized we had acquired a cat of strength and grace somewhat out of the ordinary. Of average size, he was tough and sinewy, and only in his last years did he put on a trifle too much weight. No apartment height was too difficult for him to scale, and he frequently enjoyed the avocational pastime of walking along the top edge of an open door. He played so hard that he ripped rubber balls apart and shredded the cat toys we bought him. When he used the leg of a chair in Twink's room as a scratching post, no dire punishment or threat of worse could deter him, and in virtually no time at all he reduced the chair leg to kindling.

We thought that surgery performed for the purposes of domestication might make him gentler, but it had no visible effect. He hated the "kitty doctors," as Twink called vets, and all but Dr. Harry Brown, who treated him in the last years of his life, were his enemies. He hissed and then attacked, fangs bared, when he saw a man in a white coat carrying a needle-tipped syringe.

"He's the toughest, most aggressive cat I've ever seen," a vet once told me. "If he weren't fixed he'd be a real bobcat."

We who were the members of his immediate family rarely saw the belligerent side of his nature. Although he became angry he never lost his temper, and even when badly upset he kept his sense of humor. He treated children with extraordinary care, and not once did he unsheath his claws when playing with Twink, no matter how rough she might inadvertently become.

We didn't see the steel in his nature until some friends appeared for a visit one day, bringing their German shepherd dog, Prinz, with them. I've always had great respect for German shepherds, an intelligent breed capable of killing a man—and of disposing of a mere cat without effort. Prinz was a particularly handsome specimen, about two years old, broad-shouldered, alert and powerful.

Someone hastily suggested that cat and dog be kept apart. The idea seemed wise, and I went off to lock P.J. in a bathroom, but Twink demurred. "He'll be fine, Daddy," she said. "And he won't hurt the dog if the dog behaves nicely."

By then P.J. and Prinz had spotted each other across

the living room, and both stiffened. Curious and hostile, they slowly moved toward the center of the room, while Prinz's owner and I braced ourselves for immediate intervention. Pausing, glaring, then taking another step, the animals reminded me of the principal characters in the dusty main street showdown scene of a Western. At any moment one would draw a pistol, and the fireworks would begin.

They halted about five feet apart, and stood like rigid statues. Gradually we became aware of a deep sound building inside the husky chest of the German shepherd. It was a cold, distinctly hostile sound, and didn't even remotely resemble the rumbling of a motorboat.

P.J. not only held his ground, but growled in return. I had never heard him so ferocious, so menacing.

The dog abruptly fell silent, obviously unable to believe the evidence offered him by his eyes and ears. I could scarcely blame him; I found it very difficult to believe, too.

But he recovered, advanced another foot and growled again.

P.J., refusing to yield, did the same.

By now the animals were no more than three and one-half feet apart, and it would be dangerous to separate them if one of them started a fight. One of the ladies suggested that a halt be called.

Twink was the only calm person in the room. "Oh, they won't fight," she said. "They would if one of them ran away, but they're both very brave. The dog is surprised that P.J. is so brave. They're just saying, 'Hi.'"

Her understanding soon proved superior to that of the adults. The German shepherd grew tired of exchanging insults, and stretched out on the rug. P.J., not giving an inch, sat down and yawned. Prinz scratched an ear. P.J. licked a paw. And, since no one would knock a chip off anyone else's shoulder, both became bored. Within a short time they wandered off toward different parts of the apartment, instinctively giving each other a wide berth.

Twink kept the adults informed of their whereabouts, so we were able to discuss something other than our pets. Eventually P.J. returned to tell us it was time for his dinner, and that he was hungry. The presence of a guest made it necessary to change the menu, and the moment raw hamburger appeared, so did Prinz.

I suggested taking the precaution of putting food on two plates and feeding them at opposite ends of the kitchen.

"I told you, Daddy, you don't have to," Twink said patiently. "The dog will have very good table manners, you'll see. He knows P.J. will beat him up if he doesn't."

I was so intrigued by the possibility she might be right that I decided to take the risk. Two pounds of raw, chopped meat were dumped onto a single, large dish. One tiger-striped cat and one German shepherd dog approached it from opposite sides and began to eat at the same time, each apparently unaware of the other's existence.

The dog was so hungry that, consciously or otherwise, he began to crowd his dinner companion.

P.J. didn't interrupt his meal as he emitted a single, low growl.

The German shepherd immediately gave him elbow room.

They finished at about the same time, and while P.J.

drank some milk, Prinz awaited his turn. His owners were stunned. Never, they said, had they seen him so tame in the presence of another animal; his belligerence was his greatest fault, and they kept him away from other dogs and cats so he wouldn't fight.

Both animals retired to the living room, and soon the dog sidled a trifle too close. P.J., obviously not trusting him, hissed quietly, and Prinz, flattening his ears, backed away. He remained cowed until he took his departure with his owners a short time later.

"P.J.," Twink said, hugging her Best Friend, who snuggled close to her, "is *very* fierce. I'll bet that even a real lion or tiger would be scared of him."

The rites of spring and autumn are necessary evils that city cliff dwellers must endure. Cramped for closet space, in summer they keep winter clothes in the trunks stored in apartment house basements, and in winter they keep summer clothes there. So, twice each year, they go to their dark basements, climb over dusty boxes and suitcases, then go through the ritual of unpacking and repacking.

Twink loved the cavernous basement of our apartment building, so I armed her with a flashlight and took her with me on my semiannual jaunt into the nether regions. I opened trunks, took out clothes and put away others, and meanwhile she played happily.

"Daddy," she said suddenly, her excitement intense, "I see a baby kitty." She was shining the flashlight on a small object about twenty feet away, her seven-year-old hand unsteady.

I took the flashlight from her, unwilling to tell her

that, in all probability, she had discovered a rat or mouse. She had undoubtedly found a small animal of some sort, and it was so small, so limp that I assumed it was dead. I approached it slowly, making certain Twink stayed behind me.

The creature, which was breathing, did not flee as we drew nearer.

"It's a kitty," Twink said. "Black and white."

She was right. The kitten was tiny, no more than two weeks old. He opened his eyes when we stood over him, and they were still blue.

John, the superintendent, had followed us. "There's a damn black and white mother cat in this neighborhood that makes trouble for me several times a year," he said. "She comes into my cellar to have her kittens, and then leaves them here to die."

Twink was wide-eyed. "Did his mummy go away and leave him?"

"Yes."

"Then," she said, scooping up the tiny, unprotesting creature, "he belongs to me. I'll take care of him." The matter was settled.

A quick examination by a vet assured us that the animal was suffering from no ailments, was in good health, although feeble, and would survive.

P.J. was shocked when he saw the newcomer, and protested loudly. He wanted no baby kitten entering his domain, and made his opinion known in no uncertain terms. He was so hostile, in fact, that we had to take pains to keep him away from the kitten.

That, however, was only one of our concerns. The newcomer was so tiny that, for two weeks, he had to be fed a formula of milk and sugar with an eyedropper, several times daily. We made a nest for him in a room we closed off, went to great lengths to keep P.J. out, and wondered how we had allowed ourselves to acquire another cat.

Only Twink's ecstasy prevented us from getting rid of the creature. She paid long visits to the newcomer, thereby making P.J. jealous, and she burbled interminably about the newcomer. "He can't be a Best Friend," she said. "Only P.J. and I are Best Friends. But he's a Friend. P.J. is his uncle, of course, and he's P.J.'s nephew. Unkie-dunk," she added severely to her Best Friend, who stood outside the kitten's door, growling, "be a good boy this very instant."

Not until the newcomer emerged from his isolation did Twink give serious consideration to the problem of what to call him. Until then she insisted she was "thinking about it," and had changed the subject. But now that the new four-legged member of the family was wandering around the apartment, the time had come.

"His name," she announced, "is Yum Yum."

I tried without success to conceal the intense pain that gripped me. I had always found the libretto of W. S. Gilbert's *The Mikado* cloying, and found the prospect of supporting someone called Yum Yum intolerable. "That's an awful name for a boy cat," I said.

"It happens to be his name," she said. "P.J. is P.J., and I'm Twinkie Noel-Anne. He's Yum Yum."

Soon, in self-protection, everyone else in the house referred to the new arrival as Yumsie Gumsie. It helped, but not much.

I told Twink that P.J. had to be allowed to make his

peace with the kitten in his own way, and stood by, ready to act if mayhem was threatened.

P.J. acted as though his intentions were murderous. He approached the kitten, growling and ready to spring.

The tiny animal, whose eyes were turning green now that he was a month old, blinked at his uncle in surprise. I dare say he had never imagined there could be such a huge, bristling creature in all the world.

P.J. reached out a tentative paw and took a quick swipe at the kitten.

Yum Yum tumbled over and over, then scurried under a chair.

The victory was achieved too easily, and P.J. realized his "enemy" was a product of his own imagination. He did not attack Yumsie again, ignored the smaller animal for weeks and even allowed the kitten to eat from his dish and drink from his milk bowl while he himself ate and drank. He had to be generous, Twink said, "because in our family we share things."

Not until Yumsie was about two months old did he and P.J. begin to play together. Their favorite game was race horse, and they dashed madly through the apartment, tripping humans who couldn't move out of their path quickly, occasionally knocking over ash trays and bric-a-brac. Poor Yumsie must have led a frustrated existence. P.J. had longer legs, could cover ground far more rapidly, and was infinitely more agile. When Yum Yum was chased, he was invariably caught. When he was the chaser, he couldn't come near his uncle. Yet he played the game interminably, perhaps because P.J. gave him no choice.

The experience of raising a nephew proved frustrating

for P.J., too. He jumped onto a high shelf, trying to teach Yumsie to follow his example. Little Yums always stopped a shelf or two short. P.J. soared from the floor onto the mantel over the hearth. Yumsie tried it, and crashed into the metal grill that protected the fireplace. P.J. proudly walked on the top edge of a door. Yumsie just watched.

In one department, however, the younger cat more than held his own. "He's the champion eater in this family," Twink said accurately.

Never have I seen any animal pack away meals as Yumsie did. He lived until the age of thirteen, and no matter how often he was fed, he was always ravenous. Ordinarily the cats were given two meals a day, breakfast and dinner, and P.J., the gentleman, wasn't interested in food at other times, unless there was a special tidbit being handed out.

Yumsie, however, was certain to show up the moment anyone walked into the kitchen. It became his habit to stand, looking up at the human with a begging expression in his green eyes, and, if ignored, he meeowed in a tiny voice until he was given something to eat.

He looked as though he hadn't been near a real meal, ever. He was painfully thin, his expression was woebegone, and I could count his ribs beneath his short, black and white patched fur. Yumsie never stopped eating, but remained absurdly thin all of his life.

As he matured, Yumsie developed some personality traits that were, to put it mildly, odd. He was attuned to an invisible world of his own, and could hear and see things that did not exist for others. Several times daily he stalked through the apartment, carefully, slowly placing one foot ahead of another, walking delicately and silently, peering ahead and to each side.

His behavior sometimes puzzled P.J., who saw him stalking, sat up to see what fun and games were brewing, and then dropped off to sleep again when he realized that Yumsie's overly vivid imagination was at work again. Yum Yum, however, was in earnest when he stalked. There were no enemies, four-legged or otherwise, in a Manhattan apartment, but Yumsie didn't know it. Perhaps, as we discovered when his personality underwent a drastic change after we moved to the country, he was merely practicing for what lay ahead.

Yumsie's dinosaurs were another inexplicable phenomenon. At least, that's what Twink called them after some visits to museums aroused her interest in dinosaurs, and I prefer her explanation to any other. Come to think of it, I know of no other.

Frequently, perhaps as often as once every other day, Yum Yum appeared to be walking calmly or strolling quietly through a room. His gait and attitude seemed normal, he was relaxed and, ostensibly, at peace with the world in general and P.J. in particular. Suddenly, for no discernible reason, he would leap sideways, high in the air, as though trying to escape from a huge and terrifying monster. Utterly panic-stricken, he would leave the immediate premises the instant his feet touched the floor again. Scrambling, clawing, almost literally beside himself in his desire to go elsewhere as quickly as possible, he would race into another room, dive under a bed or chair and stay there for at least a quarter of an hour, until he could assure himself that the danger no longer threatened him.

Yumsie was nine or ten months old the first time he suffered his strange hallucination, if that's what it was. Twink and I were sitting in the living room, reading, and I could scarcely believe what I had seen when he raced away. I made a thorough search, aided by Twink and P.J., but none of us could find the creature that had frightened Yumsie. I attributed the phenomenon to a noise that no one else had happened to hear, and forgot about it.

Two days later, as we were eating Sunday dinner, the incident was repeated in the dining room, and we watched in astonishment as Yumsie scurried away. P.J., who was sitting on the floor near Twink, waiting for a morsel or two of meat, paid no attention to his nephew.

"What do you suppose that was?" I asked.

Twink had been spending forty-eight hours pondering. "A dinosaur," she said.

I tried to remain unflustered. "Oh?"

"Yumsie," she said, "has a pet dinosaur. He's a very nice dinosaur. They make good pets because they're so gentle, and they only eat things like grass and oats, the way horses do."

I murmured something, I have no notion what.

"But dinosaurs are very big," she continued, warming to the theme. "And sometimes they're rough, even though they don't mean to be. Yumsie and his dinosaur play very nicely, but every once in a while the dinosaur forgets how big he is, and then Yumsie has to jump out of the way so he doesn't get stepped on. It would be awful to be stepped on by a dinosaur."

I agreed it would be catastrophic.

"Yumsie," Twink said, "doesn't have to run off and

73

hide, of course. The dinosaur feels sorry he was rough. But Yumsie is so little he doesn't know that. He gets scared, and he hides until the dinosaur says he's sorry and promises he'll be a good boy."

Yum Yum kept his pet dinosaur all of his life. The brains of dinosaurs are notoriously small, unfortunately, and they simply can't remember anything at all from one minute to the next. So Yumsie had to remain alert to avoid being crushed. He could have traded in the dinosaur for a smaller pet, I suppose, but he was too kind and gentle to be cruel to a loving creature that depended on him.

Over the years I discussed Yum Yum's dinosaur complex with various cat experts, including several veterinarians. No one pretended to know why he behaved as he did, or came up with as much as an approximation of a reasonable diagnosis. So we continued to accept Twink's theory, which was as good as any.

P.J., the pragmatist, couldn't be bothered with Yumsie's dinosaur, but on occasion he became very upset when someone in the family made too much of a fuss over Yumsie himself. Yumsie, who was merely a Friend, had no right to feel or show jealousy, and knew his place, accepting it with his quiet grace. P.J., however, never lost consciousness of his favored position as a Best Friend.

His reaction depended on the degree and extent of the attention paid his nephew. If Yumsie jumped onto someone's lap and either snuggled there or chewed on a shirt button, one of his favorite pastimes, P.J. was tolerant. After all, everyone was entitled to a fair share of love. But if someone, particularly Twink, stroked Yumsie at length, cooing at him, there was trouble.

P.J. first indicated that he was hurt by walking in a circle around the chair in which the offenders were sitting. He didn't deign to speak, presumably on the principle that a discussion of such matters was superfluous. His tail bushy, his head high, he walked slowly, with great dignity, for several minutes. If that didn't do the trick, he climbed onto the nearest chair and glared. All cats have the ability to stare at someone or something for long periods without wavering, and P.J. was a professional staring champion.

The first time I became aware of his jealousy, I watched him march around the couch on which Twink was sitting, making a fuss over Yum Yum. The march failing to bring the desired results, P.J. placed himself at the opposite end of the couch and glared stonily until Twink became aware of him.

"You know I love you, Peejus," she said. "Shame on you for being jealous!"

"*Enh, enh, enh,*" P.J. said in a hurt voice, and left the room.

V

THE CALL OF THE WILD

I shall always remember a brief incident that took place in 1950. The late Edward R. Murrow and I often encountered each other at a Manhattan nursery school, where we picked up our respective children when mothers and nursemaids were otherwise occupied. On this particular day, as we waited for our children and watched them at play, we discussed the sorry state of the world that, five years after the end of World War II, was in such turbulent disarray.

On June 25 the Korean War had erupted, and the differences that separated the West and East had become so aggravated that the future of civilization again was threatened. In fact, that morning's headlines had been devoted to a speculation by Leo Szilard, the nuclear physicist, that all human life on our planet might be extinguished by hydrogen bombs within ten to fifteen years.

I was in a gloomy mood, but Ed, so often a professional Cassandra, revealed a hardheaded optimism as he grasped my arm. "You and I don't matter a damn," he said. "But if we can do the right job on our kids, maybe they can succeed where our generation is still failing. We owe it to humanity as well as to our children themselves to give them every break."

I thought of Ed's words several years later, soon after Twink's eighth birthday, when I finally bought a house in the sleepy town of Waterford, Connecticut, near New London. A little girl could play in open fields and wade in her own brook, swim at a beach only a long stone's throw away and hike through deep woods. New York's advantages were obvious, but city life was confining, and the time had come for a change.

In June the movers came, and off we went in a huge, ancient station wagon I'd bought from Guy Sorel and Mary Jane Higby, as fine an actor and actress as ever I've known, and wonderful friends. Various household items we hadn't trusted to the ministrations of the movers were tucked away in the station wagon, among them the chiming, eight-day clock that had belonged to my father, and the flourishing indoor plants of which I was so proud.

Tucked away in a kitty cage at the back end of the station wagon were the Friends. Yum Yum accepted the situation with good-natured resignation, curled up at the rear of the cage and enjoyed a nap. P.J., however, was furious. He resented being caged, particularly with Yumsie, he disliked the noise and odors of motor vehicles and he missed the comforts of life he expected as his due.

For three solid, uninterrupted hours, from the moment I put the cage in the station wagon until I removed it beneath bushes blooming with our very own rambler roses, P.J. howled. Completely forgetting that he was a gentleman, totally indifferent to the sensitivities of others, he complained at the top of his voice. I tried to reason with him, and my wife made attempts to soothe him. Twink climbed over various fragile objects at her peril and theirs so she could sit near the cage and comfort him.

But he refused to be consoled, and continued to protest at the top of his lungs. The day was warm, the car windows were open and whenever we stopped at a traffic light, other motorists stared at us open-mouthed. I couldn't blame them. P.J.'s voice sounded like that of a young woman being subjected to intense physical torture by the Inquisition.

He forgot his travail, however, when he emerged from the cage, sniffing and cautiously moving around his new home. Within a few minutes he, Twink, and Yumsie were racing from attic to cellar and back, all of them intoxicated by the vast, unaccustomed spaces. The Friends were given their dinner, their dishes and food having been carried in the station wagon for the purpose, and we went off to a motel for the night. Diplomacy was required, as was a show of paternal firmness, to pry Twink away from her pets.

She insisted they would be lonely in the new house,

and she hugged them at length, assuring them we'd return early in the morning, before she consented to leave. The next day she was dressed before dawn, ready to return to them.

The movers came and went, and we were invaded by an army of carpenters and electricians, plumbers and painters. The adults struggled through the initiation rites known to millions of American householders, and somehow survived. Meanwhile Twink and the Friends learned the joys of country living.

Twink was afraid that the cats, if allowed to leave the house, wouldn't return. But I assured her, in spite of private misgivings, that there would be no problem. We would give the "kitty call"—a loud, repeated p-s-s-s-t—when it was time for their dinner, and they would appear.

She accepted Daddy's word, and let them out the cellar door. They crossed the terrace and started down the long, green slope to the brook, or Twinkie River, as we called it for years. Yumsie, convinced he was walking on greased glass, moved very cautiously and slowly, observing and testing, taking no chances. But P.J. apparently had convinced himself that the unknown held no terrors for him. He trotted confidently, treading on the first grass his feet had ever touched, then stopped to scratch experimentally at the bark of a towering yellow maple. No one watching him would have guessed that he was a city boy tasting a new environment for the first time.

About an hour later I paused in my grueling task of sorting and putting away books in my new study, a large, separate building located between the main house and the brook. Hearing exuberant laughter, I looked out of the windows in the direction of the swing left behind by the children of the previous owners.

P.J. was perched on the seat, his expression smug, his long whiskers bristling. Twink was pushing the swing, and when it achieved enough momentum she jumped onto the seat and rode with P.J. Both were having the time of their lives. Yumsie, who stood about ten paces from them, was staring at the branch of a beech tree, a study in concentration. He was watching a pair of robins, the first birds he had ever seen, and there was a thoughtful, somewhat dreamy look in his eyes.

I was unwilling to admit I was apprehensive, but early that evening I accompanied Twink as she went out into the yard to summon the Friends with the kitty call. To my infinite relief they appeared at once, running, Yumsie from the direction of the brook, P.J. from the heavy foliage of a gully adjoining our property. Yum Yum seemed somewhat less lugubrious than usual after his first romp in the fresh air; he was even hungrier than usual, and dashed past us, up the cellar stairs to the kitchen and his waiting dinner.

But P.J. was in no hurry. Knowing Twink wanted to hear about his adventures, he paused, rubbed against her leg and, talking at his mile-a-minute clip, told her the strange things he had seen. It was evident that he had been busy. There were several burrs imbedded in his fur, and a long stalk of dried grass was defying gravity by balancing near the nape of his neck. He was supremely happy, the country squire who had come into his own, and he swaggered as he escorted Twink to dinner.

Over a period of time the cats, P.J. in particular, had acquired a number of auxiliary names. Twink, depending on her mood and his, called him Unkie-dunk, Peejus, Mr. Brownie Nose, Mr. Boy, P.J. Ginton, Gints, Gintsie, Handsome Whiskers and a host of others. Yumsie, far more retiring, rarely inclined to show off or otherwise call attention to himself, was given relatively few auxiliary names. One, however, came into being almost spontaneously: Yum Yum the Killer.

Odd though it seemed, the shy and gentle Yumsie was a hunter with a sure instinct for game. His trophies were innumerable, and he brought most of them home, depositing them on the side-porch steps. He caught and killed so many moles that we had the only property in the neighborhood free of the pests. Once he caught a weasel, and twice he brought home drooping garter snakes. Luckily for all of us, he had the good sense to avoid skunks, and he also made it his business to give large dogs a wide berth.

Much to our distress, he was also a bird catcher, and killed more than I care to remember. It was useless to remonstrate with him, as he didn't understand why he was being scolded, and we tried to steel ourselves to his bird haul. His technique, which I witnessed on two occasions, was remarkable: he stood very still, not a muscle or whisker moving, and waited for a bird to come within reach. Then he shot into the air, a black and white streak, and brought down his prey. I wouldn't have believed it of Yumsie if I hadn't seen him in action myself.

When I discovered there were mice living in the little cellar of my study, it seemed right and natural to call on Yum Yum the Killer to relieve the situation. So I carried him to the cellar, put him inside and closed the door.

A half-hour later I returned to see what he had accomplished. There were mice scampering in the cellar, and Yumsie was there, too, his basic nature having reasserted itself. To my astonishment he sat contentedly, licking a quivering, badly frightened mouse that was afraid to move.

A firmer hand was needed, so I removed Yumsie, then asked P.J. for help. I went off to the house, returning in due time to the study cellar, where I found the Best Friend curled up on top of an old oil heater I hadn't yet removed. The mice had vanished; there was no sign of them anywhere, and they never returned. But on the far side were the remains of two large, recently killed rats. The evidence indicated that P.J. had made short work of them, disposing of each in a single attack that must have been as swift as it was brutal.

We realized, soon after we had moved to the country, that P.J.'s experience with the German shepherd dog in our New York apartment had not been an isolated incident. There were a number of dogs living in our neighborhood, most of them defying town law by roaming at will. Yumsie wisely avoided them. He fled when he saw one coming, either dashing onto the terrace, or, if he couldn't reach it in time, scurrying up the nearest tree. He was so fleet of foot that he was never in any real danger from them.

Neither was P.J., but for other reasons. The dogs knew better than to tangle with him. On scores of occasions I've seen a large dog avoid our yard because P.J. was playing or napping there. And one day Twink and two of her new classmates excitedly told me they had seen him chase a large collie down to the brook. All three stories were identical: the collie was racing furiously to get away, they said, with P.J. in hot pursuit, and the dog escaped by swimming across the brook, while P.J. stood on the near bank, triumphant, watching him.

The tale sounds too good to be true, the figment of a proud Best Friend's childish imagination. But, knowing P.J., I'm not so sure. I wouldn't put it past him.

One neighborhood dog became P.J.'s friend and companion. Candy, a lively hound with a doleful face, belonged to a little girl who lived nearby, and, like P.J., enjoyed the company of all youngsters. The two animals saw each other frequently on their excursions in fields and patches of woods. They never quarreled, and on occasion made joint investigations of birds nesting overhead. It wasn't unusual, either, for Candy to visit us when he was thirsty, and P.J. never protested when the dog drank from his milk or water bowl.

Often P.J. and Candy went off together to share another, more exciting adventure. Twink reported seeing them duck watching on the bank of the cove owned by Jim and Pat Fox. Jim, the Electric Boat Company's crackerjack, trouble-shooting technical writer, is an honest man, and said he'd never seen the sight. Pat, who writes and illustrates children's books under the name of Patricia Coombs, is endowed with a strong streak of whimsy. So I listened somewhat skeptically when she assured me, with a straight face, that Twink's account was truthful.

I do know that P.J. was fascinated by ducks. There are scores of them who come to the cove every spring, and one pair, a handsome drake and his mate, made regular excursions up our brook, which flows into the cove. Twink discovered them on our hill one spring day, and was given some bread to feed them. That was the beginning of what I believe to be an unusual relationship.

Daily, for more than two months, Mr. and Mrs. Duck-duck, as Twink called them, came to us to be fed. Twink faithfully brought them bread, which she broke into small pieces, and they became so tame they climbed to the top of the hill and stood outside the terrace door. Toward the end of their stay they rewarded her fidelity by parading up the brook with their ducklings, Mr. Duck-duck in the lead, his wife behind him, the three babies in single file bringing up the rear.

What I find remarkable is that Mr. and Mrs. Duck-duck have returned every year for a springtime visit. Twink is grown now, a married woman with a family and home of her own, but still the ducks come. Michele, my second daughter, eagerly took over the responsibility of feeding Mr. and Mrs. Duck-duck the year Twink went off to college, and now Margot, my youngest daughter, clamors to get into the act, too.

Admittedly I know nothing about wild or semi-wild ducks. I have no idea how long they live or anything else about them. So I can't be positive the same pair have come—and are still coming—for the annual visit. To this day Twink swears our visitors are Mr. and Mrs. Duck-duck, and that she can identify them by their markings. Michele, who, I must interject, believes anything Twink says is Gospel, seconds the claim. Rightly or wrongly, I have reservations, and won't blame the reader who chooses to raise a jaundiced eyebrow.

I do know, however, that the ducks preyed on P.J.'s

mind. He watched them daily from the terrace or a vantage point near our favorite white pine on the hill. He
growled and bristled, perhaps because he was jealous
when he watched Twink feed them, perhaps because he
was opposed to ducks on general principles.

One day, after the visit of Mr. and Mrs. Duck-duck
had extended more than six weeks, P.J. decided the situation had become intolerable. He paced up and down
restlessly as Twink fed them their bread, and I had an
idea that something out of the ordinary was brewing. My
hunch was right.

As Twink and I stood at the crest of the hill, watching,
Mr. and Mrs. Duck-duck slowly waddled down to the
brook. P.J. followed, stalking them, at first carefully remaining about ten paces behind them. If they were aware
of his presence they did not indicate it by as much as
the ruffling of a single feather.

Gradually P.J. crept closer, then closer still. By the time
the ducks reached the bank of the brook he was no more
than three paces behind them. He crouched, ready to
spring, and Twink became very upset.

But P.J. became far more upset. Mr. Duck-duck turned,
and, spreading his large wings, flapped them wildly and
honked in a deep *basso profundo*.

Never, before or since, did I see P.J. react to a situation
with such alacrity. He whirled and sped up the hill, his
ears plastered close to his head, his bushy tail extended
straight behind him. Not once did he hesitate, not once
did he turn to see if the drake was following him. The
flapping of those giant wings and the honking of that
deep voice had been enough to convince him that he
wanted to be elsewhere.

Twink had the presence of mind to jerk the terrace door open, which was fortunate, as P.J. would have crashed through the screening in order to escape. He fled through the cellar, up to the main floor, then up another flight to Twink's suite. She followed, and after a search found him under the far end of her bed. Nothing would coax him to come out, and he remained there for the rest of the day, not budging until hunger impelled him to return to the kitchen for his dinner.

Thereafter he took care to avoid Mr. and Mrs. Duck-duck. Neither that year nor any other year did he acknowledge their presence on our property. When they appeared for their daily meal of bread, P.J. decided to take himself to more interesting places for more absorbing activities. After all, any idiot could watch ducks, and there wasn't much fun in that.

When I asked Twink if P.J. still accompanied Candy down to the cove for some idle duck-watching, she merely grinned at me.

More than anything else, country living gave P.J. unending opportunities to indulge his love of heights. It became commonplace to find him roaming on the roof of my study, which he could reach from a nearby oak. Occasionally we found him on the roof of the house itself, and didn't know how he got there until Twink discovered that he had found a way to loosen a screen in the window of her room that opened onto the roof.

Trees, however, were far more fun than roofs. We have several towering oaks on the property, as well as a number of handsome maples, a few ordinary beech and one lovely willow. P.J. became familiar with all of them, and spent at least a portion of each day climbing to dizzy heights. He experimented, briefly, with the evergreens, but found them too prickly and sticky. Once he made a flying leap onto the trunk of the white pine, when it was a fairly small tree, but retreated quickly, a dozen or more long, drooping needles protruding from his fur. He did not try the experiment again, but earned himself a new auxiliary name, Mr. Porcupine.

Squirrels, more than any other country creatures, irritated P.J. He considered them fair game, and wanted to catch them, or at least play with them, but they were too agile for him. Disinclined to take unnecessary risks with a tiger-striped monster several times their size, they invariably fled at his approach, leaping from branch to branch, and, on occasion, from tree to tree in order to get away from him.

Our oaks attracted a great many of the neighborhood squirrels in the early autumn, when the acorns started dropping, and my work was often interrupted by the thudding of acorns and scurrying of squirrels on my study roof. The activities of the squirrels fascinated and infuriated P.J., and one October day the challenge became unbearable.

I was returning to my study after lunch when I saw him climbing the adjacent oak, and I paused to watch his acrobatics. The squirrels were far above him, cavorting and, perhaps, taunting him, and his no-nonsense attitude made it plain that he intended to teach them a lesson. He followed, far higher than I had ever seen him climb, until he reached thin, supple branches that bent perilously beneath his weight. I realized he had discarded all caution in his desire to reach the squirrels, so

I called him, urging him to come down, but he paid no attention to me.

Suddenly, as the branch on which he was standing swayed and dipped, it occurred to him that he had gone too far. He tested his footing, then froze.

I tried to coax him down, but extreme caution had replaced daring, and he made no move.

Residents of larger communities than ours call the fire department in such emergencies, but we have only volunteer firemen, and I've never heard of anyone asking them to leave their jobs for the purpose of rescuing an animal in distress. So I had to do what I could myself.

I hurried off to the cellar for my cumbersome, fifteen-foot ladder, struggled out into the open with it and propped it against the tree. Then, in spite of my own troubles with heights, I climbed to the top rung, trying to soothe the frightened P.J. and coax him down. By now he was regretting his rash behavior, and refused to compound it by taking any more chances. He remained on the same branch, so intent on his own dilemma that he was no longer aware of the chattering squirrels enjoying the spectacle of his humiliation.

When I saw I was getting nowhere with him, I knew I needed an aid of some sort to entice him sufficiently to make him forget his terror. I thought a piece of meat might do the trick, and went off to the kitchen. A light dawned as I opened the refrigerator: some friends had given us a large venison steak, which we had cooked the previous evening, but hadn't found to our taste. I found it in the refrigerator and returned to the ladder, waving the slab of greasy meat as I once more mounted to the top rung.

P.J. was interested in spite of his fear. His nose twitched, his ears became very pointed and he gazed longingly at the steak. I continued to coax, waving it, and at last he started his descent. It took him the better part of an hour to make his way down the network of branches to a point just beyond my reach, and there, inexplicably, he halted. Crouching on a relatively stable fork, he continued to look at the meat but remained immobile.

I talked until I became hoarse. The hard wood of the ladder rung cut through the soles of my soft moccasins, and my feet ached. I was becoming dizzier by the minute, and was afraid I might fall to the ground if I allowed myself to look down. I gladly would have made a free gift of my charming country house to the first person who came along, and would have been delighted to move back to the city.

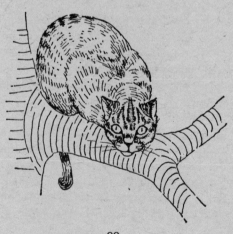

Eventually my patience deserted me. "P.J.," I said, "you're stupid! If you want to spend the rest of the day and the night there, that's your business, but I have a living to earn and other things to do. Goodbye."

I moved down one rung, intending to return to the ground.

P.J. meeowed, gathered himself and leaped.

He was expecting me to catch him, I'm sure, but his sudden move caught me off guard. Somehow I managed to grasp him with one hand while clinging simultaneously to the ladder and the venison with the other, and miraculously the force of his thrust didn't send both of us hurtling to the ground. P.J. dug in for dear life, his claws cutting through my sweater and shirt, lacerating my shoulder.

The pain was excruciating, but at last we made our way to safety. Both of us were exhausted, and limped into the house. I had no desire to reward P.J., but felt I had to give him some of the meat so he wouldn't lose confidence in my promises. I cut several small chunks for him, and, while he ate it, poured myself a stiff drink.

By the next day he was happily climbing trees again, but had learned a lesson. Now he merely went beyond the heights that a less acrobatic cat would dare approach, but he resolutely closed his eyes, ears and mind to the squirrels responsible for his degradation.

It was just a short time later that I saw an astonishing sight. Twink and P.J. were enjoying a frolic together in the yard, and a pair of squirrels, gathering acorns, moved to a spot no more than five feet from the Best Friends. P.J. refused to admit they existed. Ignoring their chatter, he concentrated on the ball attached to a long string that

Twink was pulling through dead leaves. It was obvious that squirrels had become creatures he could take or leave alone, preferably the latter.

The differences between country and city living become painfully apparent in winter. I hadn't yet put permanent, aluminum storm windows on the house, and spent a chilly weekend hoisting the old-fashioned storm windows into place. Raw winds howled through the shutters, and the fur of the Friends grew thick, even though they were increasingly reluctant to spend more than short periods outdoors.

P.J., however, allowed nothing to prevent him from going through his morning ritual of accompanying Twink to the school bus stop, which was the equivalent of a city block away. No matter what the weather he trotted beside her, and would not be deterred by heavy, late autumn rains or a vicious sleet storm. Escorting his Best Friend to her bus was his job, and he took the responsibility seriously.

Our house is heated by an old-fashioned gravity-flow system, with heat pouring up from the cellar furnace through a large metal grate located at the junction of our living room, kitchen and radio-television-record player room, which we call the music room. Even in warm weather P.J. didn't trust the grate, and when going from one room to another daintily made his way along its edge. I was always surprised by the speed he could achieve in this maneuver.

Yum Yum was not in the least disturbed by the grate, which seemed contrary to his basic character. And when heat started to pour up through the grate, Yumsie discovered heaven on earth. He quickly developed the new habit of stretching out on it, luxuriating in the heat. The colder the weather the longer he stayed there, sometimes sleeping for hours.

I still don't know how he could tolerate such extreme heat. The metal of the grate was uncomfortable when touched by the bare foot of a human, but Yumsie proved himself to be unexpectedly tough and resilient. When Twink came in from the cold she enjoyed standing on the grate, but after spending a maximum of five minutes there she had enough. Yumsie was baked, roasted and parboiled, I'm sure, but in subzero weather I've seen him spend a whole day on the grate without suffering any ill effects.

When the Friends saw their first country snowfall they became wildly excited. Twink put on gear appropriate for the day, and went out to make a snowman with some classmates. I cursed, climbed into my boots and shoveled the white stuff from my horseshoe-shaped driveway, which is located on a slope. By the following morning the snow was deep outside the terrace, and Twink decided the time had come for the Friends to taste the delights of winter.

Yumsie experimentally took a single step outside the open terrace door. He dipped a front paw into the snow, snatched himself away and resolutely returned to the house, determined to have no part of the nasty, wet blanket.

P.J., of course, was made of sterner stuff. His initial test was similar to Yumsie's, and he, too, recoiled. But he tried a second time, then a third. Meanwhile Twink was urging him to join her in the snow.

I didn't want her to be disappointed, and told her he wouldn't, as he was congenitally opposed to the discomforts of wet fur.

"He likes snow!" Twink declared. "Can't you tell?"

I couldn't frankly, but she understood him, as always. He gathered himself for a flying leap, and a moment later landed in a bank of powdery snow. Then he plowed forward to reach Twink, only his head and part of his tail showing above snow-line. The Best Friends played for an hour or more, and not until they returned to the house did P.J. realize, as the snow melted, that he was as bedraggled as Twink. She dried him with a large towel before going off to change her clothes.

He was still enough of a city dweller and aesthete to realize that a little snow went a long way, and it wasn't often that she could lure him out into the cold. When the weather was at its worst, P.J., like any sensible man, preferred to curl up near a good book or two.

It was the following winter, I believe, that an ice storm completely glazed roads, yards and fields, coating the bare branches of trees. Twink had been given a new sled for Christmas, and couldn't be dissuaded from trying it out on our hill. P.J. and I went as far as the terrace to watch; the footing was so slick and treacherous that neither of us was willing to venture into the open.

But Twink happily climbed onto her sled and started down the slope. She shouted exuberantly, but the sound died away before she had traveled more than twenty or thirty feet. She was gaining momentum far more rapidly than she had imagined possible, and soon the sled was out of control. It whipped down the hill, shot out over the bank and landed with a crash on the frozen brook.

The crust of ice wasn't thick enough to withstand the impact of the child-bearing sled, and Twink, who was drenched, found herself standing in chilly, waist-deep water. P.J. meeowed, but had the sense not to leave the terrace. I shouted and started down the hill.

Sheer luck prevented me from skidding all the way down the slope and landing in the brook myself. Twice I lost my balance; once a laurel bush halted me, and then I crashed into a clump of arbor vitae. Meanwhile Twink had dragged herself and the sled out of the brook and had started up the hill. But her clothes froze, and the coating of ice on them made it doubly difficult for her to negotiate the incline.

Slipping, falling, and slipping again, she struggled up toward the top as I, still unable to keep my balance, half-worked and half-skidded toward her. It took us at least a quarter of an hour to reach the terrace together, and by that time Twink was turning blue.

P.J., talking rapidly, greeted his Best Friend as she reached safety. Then, not waiting an instant, he turned and raced to the cellar door, leading her to the hot bath and steaming cup of cocoa that awaited her. While she soaked in the tub he stood outside the bathroom door, still jabbering, alternately scolding and worrying aloud. When she emerged he accompanied her to her room for clean, dry clothes, dashing ahead of her up the stairs, then doubling back to nuzzle her before showing her the way again.

For the rest of the day he literally refused to leave her side. He jumped to a kitchen chair near her when she drank her steaming cocoa, showing no interest in the snacks he was offered. She moved to the living room, where she sat on a sofa, covered with a blanket, and P.J. hovered over her, jumping onto the couch and rubbing against her, talking and dropping to the floor for a few minutes before repeating the process.

That night he refused to eat his dinner until she came into the kitchen, and when he finally went to his plate he kept watching her, ready to leave if she did. He spent the night on her bed, and not until the following morning, when we knew for certain that the experience had done her no harm, did he relax and stop acting as her ever-present guardian. He, like Twink, did not wear the mantle of a Best Friend lightly.

VI

THE EXPANDING CIRCLE OF FRIENDS

One rainy autumn day about fifteen months after we had moved to the country a very damp black and white kitten with the most intense, clear green eyes I have ever seen followed Twink home from the school bus stop. He was about six months old and so painfully thin that he made Yumsie look like a Swiss banker. Perhaps some of the neighborhood animals had told him we were partial to cats in our house, or it may be that he sensed an instinctive sympathy in Twink.

Whatever his reasons, he walked close behind her, meeowing, and she, to be sure, paused frequently to pat

97

him. "There's a hungry little kitty outside," she announced as she came into the house.

P.J. and Yumsie, sleek, well-fed and dry, jumped up to the kitchen counter window overlooking the side door and growled.

I agreed to let Twink bring the kitten inside to be fed, but the Friends created such an uproar that the food dish had to be moved out to the yard. The ravenous little beast ate every crumb, and returned that evening for more.

The weather worsened overnight, and a hard, driving rain heralded the beginning of a typical three-day New England nor'easter. But the soaked kitten was waiting outside the kitchen door when Twink came downstairs to give the Friends their breakfast. Her heart went out to the stranger, and she lectured P.J. and Yumsie severely, telling them they were selfish brutes. Then she brought the kitten into the house and stood guard to make sure he wasn't attacked.

P.J. and Yum Yum were so angry they retired from the scene, P.J. complaining bitterly. The kitten, with the kitchen to himself, ate a large breakfast and drank the better part of a bowl of milk. Twink dried him with a towel, kept him beside her as she ate her own breakfast and then took him up to her room with her while she prepared for school.

Belatedly I realized that the cat population in our house had increased, and that morning I took the newcomer off to the vet for shots and an examination. The Friends growled at him when I brought him home, but he was tough after making his way in the world and threatened them in return. He gave almost as good as he received, and had to be rescued only a few times. P.J. became almost inarticulate when the kitten quietly climbed the stairs to Twink's room, where he made himself at home and took a nap.

Twink expected him to be there, and wasn't in the least surprised to see him when she came home that afternoon. "His name," she told me, "is Mostly Black and White Meeower."

I was too weak from shock to utter more than a faint protest. "That's too long a name."

"He wants us to call him Mostly," she said.

Yumsie showed unexpected realism by accepting what the fates had ordained, and gave up the fight. Within forty-eight hours he and Mostly were sleeping only inches apart on the heater grill. Perhaps there is something in the metabolism of black and white cats that enables them to enjoy, much less tolerate, intense heat up from the oil furnace. Whatever the reason, Mostly became fond of the heater, and soon was spending long periods on the grill. Unlike Yumsie, however, he knew when he'd had enough.

P.J. found Mostly intolerable, and could not be induced to change his opinion. He raised such a row at feeding time that, for many weeks, the kitten was compelled to wait until P.J. finished a meal before being allowed to approach the feeding dish. But Mostly had a will of his own, and day by day edged closer to the dish at mealtimes. P.J. pretended he wasn't there, and eventually they were eating from the same dish, standing side by side.

That, however, was the extent of their mutual tolerance. They lived under the same roof for more than a decade, and never did they become friends, never did they play together. They might sleep at arm's length on the same bed or sofa, but if Mostly approached closer, P.J.'s growl warned him that he was trespassing.

When Mostly—sometimes called "Mr. Eek-eek"—became full grown he decided to test his strength, and the whole household was awakened one morning before dawn by a vicious, snarling fight. By the time I dragged myself out of bed and chased the culprits, the fight had ended. P.J. was unscathed, but Mostly had several long, deep scratches across his nose that required medication. That dispute was a foretaste of things to come.

For the rest of their lives, P.J. and Mostly mixed it up at least once each week. Mostly was a real glutton for punishment, and almost always suffered scratches or bites on the head and face. Occasionally he also scored, and P.J. carried some scars as reminders of an encounter. Neither could be persuaded to stop, however, and we found no way to induce them to bury their hatchets.

When Twink scolded them, Mostly's reaction was sheepish. He stared at her, his green eyes intense, then rubbed against her leg and began to rumble. P.J., on the other hand, neither felt sorry nor was willing to apologize. He was quick enough to repent other misdeeds, like his trick of ripping a box of paper tissues to tiny shreds, and could be shamed into begging his mistress' forgiveness before repeating the crime. But when Twink lectured him for fighting with Mostly, he became bored and walked away. We consoled ourselves with the thought that at least he was honest and wouldn't pretend.

In the months immediately following Mostly's arrival, P.J. taught himself to turn on the cold water tap in the kitchen sink, pushing it with a paw, and then drinking from it. I am tempted to accept Twink's claim: the water dish was small, and Mostly was a thirsty kitten who spent a great deal of time at the dish. Therefore, Twink said, P.J. learned to drink from the tap so be wouldn't have to associate with the newcomer. A desire to write a truthful report makes it impossible for me to say that Twink's theory was accurate. So I must confine myself to the observation that P.J. did indeed turn on the tap and drink from it.

Unfortunately, he never bothered to learn how to turn the tap off after he had used it. Our water comes from our own well, which makes us dependent on seasonal rainfalls, and for many years New England has been suffering from summer droughts. Once, two or three years after we had moved to the country, we "went dry" for forty-eight hours, a thoroughly unpleasant experience we were determined not to suffer again. So we adopted strict water conservation measures every summer, and only P.J. ignored them. Frequently we returned from an outing to find precious water pouring into the kitchen sink. I tightened the fixtures in an attempt to halt his practice, but he was strong enough—and clever enough—to outwit me.

Mostly enjoyed water, too, in a different way that I have found unique in cats. When the Friends left the house every morning for their day's adventures in the open, Mostly almost always headed for his favorite romping ground on the far side of the brook. In order to reach the field, of course, he had to cross the brook. In the summer months, when the stream was very low, he disdainfully waded across, indifferent to his own splashing. In spring and fall, when the water was deeper and the brook spread to a width of about six or seven feet, he swam.

His fur was wet when he came home at the end of the day, making it necessary to dry him in the cellar before allowing him to proceed into the rest of the house. Sometimes he eluded the towel-bearer, and left muddy tracks on floors, rugs and furniture. Mostly was not the favorite pet of our cleaning women.

He had the good sense to avoid the brook after a heavy rainfall, when it became a swirling torrent, and nothing could have persuaded him to go near it in winter. Like Yumsie, Mostly hated the cold, and sensibly refused to leave the house in raw, chilly weather.

Since he had been a stray, accustomed to roaming the neighborhood, we wondered whether he might disappear when we first allowed him to leave the house. But Mostly, having known privation, had no intention of starving or suffering discomfort again. When Twink went out into the yard and gave the kitty call, summoning the Friends to a meal, he was the first to appear.

It was Mostly's insatiable appetite that proved his undoing. In later years increasingly heavy traffic on the road outside our house, which resulted in the death of other people's pets, forced us to keep the Friends indoors at all times, a practice we follow down to the present day. P.J. came within a fraction of an inch of being run over one evening when he raced home in response to Twink's call, an incident that frightened us badly and made us determined to take no more unnecessary chances.

All the cats quickly became accustomed to permanent indoor living, and Mostly, more than the others, gave in to a life of slothful indolence. His appetite remained unchanged, and the lack of outdoor exercise caused him to put on weight. We tried to diet him, but found it impossible to feed him separately; we obtained medication for him from the vet, but he confounded his doctor—and us —by continuing to grow fatter. Toward the end of his life he became grossly overweight.

In fact, he weighed twenty-eight pounds. We know because Twink stood on the scale, first with him, then without him, in order to determine his weight. He was still broad-chested and powerful, but found it too much bother to leap up onto furniture. Since he was a bed-burrower who liked to work his way under blankets, his new habits were not an unmixed blessing.

"But he still thinks he's a baby lap kitten," Twink remarked one day when Mostly made a flying leap from the floor and landed on me with a crash that raised lumps on me.

It was true that Mostly didn't think of himself as fat, and loved to curl up on an available lap. It wasn't easy to move when his weight pinned one down, but we always allowed him to stay. After all, we didn't want to hurt his feelings, and the overweight are inclined to be hypersensitive.

Pat and Jim Fox have always kept a menagerie that has made our population of Friends look puny. They're never without five to seven cats, and they're rarely without a collection of rabbits, white mice and a rare species of hamster. A turtle lived in their bathtub for three years before he (she) pined for the outdoors and was returned to the brook, deep in the woods, where he (she) had first been found. A pet skunk, de-skunked, spent several years sleeping alternately in their kitchen and cellar. And they experimented with a greeb, a ducklike creature that kept banging itself into the ends of their tub while swimming because it has eyes at the sides of its face and cannot look ahead.

Henry, a yellow tom whom Twink has always called their Chief Cat, followed Pat and Jim one evening when they came up the road to our house for a drink. Wanting conviviality and deeply resenting his exclusion, Henry sat outside our door and yowled. Ashamed of our inhospitable attitude, we rectified the error.

Henry stalked into our kitchen, heading straight for the dish of cat food, but found his path blocked by P.J. Bob Ardrey tells in his fascinating book, *The Territorial Imperative,* what happens when one Chief Cat encounters another, particularly on the latter's home ground. I grabbed P.J. and Jim got his hands on Henry before mutual mayhem was committed, and we took them, growling and struggling, to separate but adjoining rooms, shutting the door. Both tried to claw it down while exchanging violent insults and challenges, so Jim finally decided that Henry's manners weren't befitting a guest. Henry was taken outside and told to go home.

Well, he started homeward, but he took the wrong fork and wandered to the far side of the cove. There, much later in the night, he saw lights burning in his own house, wanted to go home and couldn't find his way there. So he howled, mournfully, until Pat, who had just gone to bed, got up again, dressed and went off on a safari to fetch him.

The self-imposed Fox limit of seven cats had been reached when one of the females gave birth to a litter of two superb long-haired kittens. They kept the gray, Ulysses, or 'Lissy, and gave us the golden kitten, the first of our females.

As these lines are being written, Higgeldy Piggeldy Poo has risen to the rank of Chief Cat in our house, and has acquired a decorum that matches the responsibilities of her post. Twink and I may be prejudiced, but we think she is the prettiest cat we've ever seen. Her fur is a long, fluffy mass of gold, with blending tan streaks on her haunches and the underside of her magnificently plumed tail. She has what Twink has always called a "sweet and loving" face, and there is a golden cast to her green eyes that matches her fur.

Fine-boned and dainty, she could be held in the palm of a child's hand when she first joined our family. She was friendly and uninhibited from the outset, and, having spent the first six to eight weeks in a cat-filled house, was unafraid of the huge males she encountered in her new home.

P.J., Yumsie, and Mostly went through the expected routines. They were nettled by the presence of the little intruder, and growled at her. And for twenty-four hours after she joined us, Twink and I had to make certain they kept their distance from her.

Then something out of the ordinary happened. P.J. discovered she was a female, and his attitude changed. As Twink said, "He knows she's his niece, so he wants to be nice to her and protect her."

I am strongly inclined to agree, because he did assume the role of her guardian. He played with her, gently, letting her chase him all around the house, then chasing her, adjusting his speed to that of the short-legged kitten so he wouldn't spoil their game by catching her. When

Yumsie threatened Higgeldy, P.J. put him in his place with a leap, a growl and a nip that sent Yum Yum flying. When Mostly hissed at the kitten, P.J. lunged at him, snarling, and Mostly took refuge under a bed. What impressed us most was P.J.'s courtliness at dinner. He made a place for Higgeldy beside him at the dish, and kept a wary eye on his nephews to prevent them from forgetting they were gentlemen.

Within a very short time these precautions became unnecessary. Yumsie and Mostly lost their hearts to the kitten, too, and enjoyed playing a game of tag with her. They made no protest when she joined them for meals, and tried to push her aside only when tidbits of chicken were being handed out at our dinner table.

But P.J., who had such a soft spot for her, remained her closest companion. He taught her to play follow-the-leader, and she cavorted in his wake, leaping from window sill to table to chair. From the night of her arrival Higgeldy slept on Twink's bed, and P.J. began spending longer periods there, too. Twink told me they snuggled close together when they slept, which I wouldn't believe until I saw them myself, and found her description accurate.

Yumsie and Mostly reached the conclusion that Twink's bed was the "in" place to spend a night, and it wasn't unusual to find four cats crowding one small, blissfully happy girl. P.J. and Higgeldy usually made a joint place for themselves within arm's reach, so Twink could stroke them the instant she awoke, while Yumsie and Mostly used the lower portion of the bed, Mostly making certain he didn't venture too close to P.J.

When the weekly fight between P.J. and Mostly

erupted, Yum Yum didn't want to be the innocent by-stander caught between opposing gangsters. The instant he heard the first growl that presaged trouble, he quietly took himself off to a remote, safe place, and there he stayed until the duel ended. Higgeldy, however, knew she wouldn't be dragged into the fight, and rarely stirred. Sometimes she was an interested spectator, watching as the gladiators lunged and feinted, but the rough sport of mere males was beneath her, and we've seen her remain blissfully recumbent, paying no attention to the trials of strength guaranteed to awaken the entire neighborhood.

Her feminine instinct proved a help in other ways, too. While still a kitten she discovered that "the boys," as Twink now called them, rarely paid us visits at lunch. Consequently she alone would be the beneficiary of any snacks being handed out. It is a rare day, down to the present, that she doesn't make an appearance at lunch.

As a result she long ago developed a fondness for cold meats that none of the other cats share. She is a profes-sional liverwurst eater, and she loves Hungarian salami, undeterred by the odors of garlic. Like P.J. and Mostly, however, she couldn't be induced to share Yum Yum's craving for asparagus. The moment he caught his first whiff of asparagus being cooked he appeared in the kitchen, and there he stayed, begging, until he was given a few stalks. But Yumsie, as we always said, had his odd streaks.

Twink and the newest Friend developed a very special game. Higgeldy curled around the back of Twink's neck, looking like a glorious red fox scarf, and there she stayed for long periods. It didn't matter whether Twink moved around the house, read a book or watched television. Higgeldy was content, and often fell asleep on her human perch. To this day, for old time's sake, they still play the game when the mood strikes them.

Twink and I long ago came to a parting of the ways on the question of the new kitten's name. It was Twink who called her Higgeldy Piggeldy Poo when she first arrived, of course, her talents in the field being unique. But it was inevitable that a child enthralled by A. A. Milne's Christopher Robin & associates would shorten the name to Poolet. Marilyn, my wife, calls the present Chief Cat Poolet, and so do all three of my younger children. I am a purist, however, and insist on calling her Higgeldy. When she feels like responding, she answers to either name, and she purrs when Twink calls her Golden, too. I might add that Jim Fox refers to her as Schweppes, but that's another story.

Higgeldy has one habit that has frustrated me for more than ten years. Wanting attention, she approaches a person's chair, rumbling, and after being stroked throws herself onto the floor. Then she rolls over onto her back, having discovered a long time ago that there are few joys in life as satisfying as that of having her tummy rubbed. As she hits the floor, however, she manages to roll j-u-s-t beyond the stroker's reach, a gesture that forces her admirer to half-leave his seat.

I've accommodated her on countless occasions at the cost of my own immediate comfort, only to have her repeat the process, thereby compelling me to leave my chair. I've told her she's self-centered and inconsiderate, but she's a female and doesn't listen to such talk from a man. Only recently has a light dawned, and now I use a different technique: I extend my hand, arm outstretched, and tell her she must come closer if she wants to be stroked.

In theory I've found the perfect solution, but it doesn't work out as planned. Higgeldy is far too feminine. Her golden-green eyes blink at me sorrowfully, her plumed tail waves lazily and she curls her front paws beneath her. So I heave myself out of my chair and move closer to her in order to stroke her. I guess she's learned how to handle me, because I don't really mind in the least.

One day, about a year after Higgeldy joined us, I was busily engaged in a chore I ordinarily loathe, that of painting the terrace. This time I was impervious to the aches in little-used muscles that would appear by the end of the day. Only that morning I had received a very pleasant telephone call from my agent, Oliver Swan, of the Paul Reynolds office. My new Doubleday novel, *The Conqueror's Wife*, the story of the private life of William of Normandy, had just been taken as a selection of the Literary Guild.

I splashed paint on ceiling, walls, and myself, scarcely conscious of what I was doing, when the insistent meeeow-ing of a kitten cut through my euphoric fog. I looked down to see a small animal approach me with the self-confidence of one who was aware of her beauty. She was pure white, slightly grubby at the moment, and would have been albino had her eyes not been green.

Again the neighborhood grapevine had been busy, and she realized she had found a patsy for cats. I brought a filled food dish out to the yard, and as she gobbled hun-grily, I accepted the inevitable. By the time Twink came home from school, the kitten had already been taken to the vet for shots and medication for an infection.

She also had been given a name: Guilda. It was my turn, I said firmly, and wouldn't allow the ecstatic Twink to change it. She was so happy to have another kitten that she didn't put up much of a fight.

Guilda is a bouncing, loving extrovert, a cat endowed with unquenchable high spirits and unlimited energy. No one, least of all her peers, would call her an intellectual. A hedonist among hedonists, she engages in a constant search for fun and excitement, attention and games. When she can't find another cat to play race horse, or a human to pat her, she'll sit in a window and look out at the moths and other "night creatures," as Twink has always called the insects that appear after dark.

I don't mean to indicate that Guilda isn't feminine. She is, and knows it, but is also something of a tomboy. She has a reckless quality, thumbing her nose at the world, and she's certainly no lady. This past spring, for example, her white whiskers were a bright orange for weeks after she made too close an inspection of the handiwork of our house painters. Her voice is a somewhat raucous near-baritone, reminiscent of the late Tallulah Bankhead's, and she speaks loudly, disdaining subtlety.

She has an infinite capacity for getting into mischief, but escapes with only minor damage. On one occasion, when she was a year old, something cooking in the kitchen aroused her curiosity, and she jumped up onto the stove, her tail perilously close to the adjacent electric burner, which was turned high. Twink immediately hauled her down, but in those few seconds Guilda managed to burn a long streak of hair off her tail. She neither knew nor cared; miraculously, she had escaped injury, and wasn't bothered because her appearance was marred for weeks.

Guilda doesn't have too good a memory, either. The sight of water running in the kitchen sink fascinates her, and for years she jumped up to the back of the sink, edged close to the stream and then tried to catch it with a front paw. The wet feel of water disgusted and annoyed her, however, and she invariably snatched her paw away, then jumped to the floor, meeowing angrily. Her memory was so short, unfortunately, that she reappeared a few hours later, when the sink was turned on again, and went through an identical, miserable experience.

Twink believes it isn't a faulty memory but an indifference to consequences that causes Guilda to behave as she does. "She knows the water will wet her paw," Twink said when we first discussed the phenomenon. "It's just that she loves running water so much she can't resist reaching out to touch it."

Guilda can be the most stubborn of cats, too. She is the only one of the Friends who has refused to accept the edict that my walk-in clothes closet is forbidden territory. The others tried to sneak in and taste the delights there when they thought no one was looking, but they halted when told, "Enh, enh." Guilda, however, becomes conveniently deaf and tries to dash past human legs in order to reach the interior of the closet.

She knows it is wrong to eat indoor plants, and for years dashed off to a hiding place after Twink discovered that one of the Friends had been nibbling at a plant and demanded the identity of the guilty party. But that didn't stop Guilda, and she continued to chew at the plants until we found a few years ago that she dislikes the odor of geranium plants. It isn't accidental that the largest of our present indoor plants, shielding all the others, is a geranium "tree" that stands almost four feet tall and has a branch spread of thirty-eight inches, measured by Twink.

The Friends accepted Guilda without protest or fuss, and she created the least stir of any newcomer. Yumsie and Mostly were pleased, and Higgeldy realized that Guilda, although a startling white, could not compete with her own golden beauty. P.J. was delighted that a new playmate had moved in, and within minutes after Guilda's arrival he was playing race horse with her.

This pastime in no way resembled the gentle game of tag he played with Higgeldy. He and Guilda raced at full tilt through the house, whipping up and down stairs, sprinting through rooms. They knocked over wastebaskets, upset bric-a-brac, crashed into people and sent small objects spinning. They played until Guilda was exhausted and threw herself onto the floor, panting, her tongue hanging out. P.J. tried her stamina to the utmost, but the moment she recovered she was ready for another round.

Guilda's athletic prowess was—and is—unusual. Twink, watching her clear the top of a long coffee table in a superb high hurdle exhibition, once remarked, "She isn't a kitty, Daddy. I think she's a kangaroo, or maybe an antelope."

Guilda's boldness most nearly resembled P.J.'s, but the unknown sometimes frightens her and causes her to shrink. A butterfly fluttering on the terrace made her apprehensive, and she avoided it, although she unhesitatingly attacked strange cats that wandered onto our property. But instinct was responsible, I believe, when a hornet, buzzing angrily, managed to get into the house one summer day. She has always been fascinated by the sounds that insects make, but she wanted nothing to do with the hornet, who was no ordinary night creature. She took herself to the snug haven of the kitty house, a box on the stair landing between the kitchen and cellar, and left me to get a bug spray.

There was a distinct limit to the camaraderie the Friends shared with Guilda. She was one of them, enjoying all privileges of the club—until mealtime. "The boys" adamantly refused her permission to approach the food plate while they ate, and made no exceptions. P.J. was even more firm in his insistence that she obey the rule than were Yumsie and Mostly. It didn't matter that he had been playing with her five minutes earlier, and would resume the game immediately after dinner. While P.J. ate, Guilda waited, and if she had the temerity to approach the plate prematurely, he drove her away.

There wasn't room for more than four cats to eat out of the same dish at one time, and I thought Twink made sense when she asked me to buy a larger plate for the Friends. I did, but the situation remained unchanged. Guilda sat nearby, longingly, until the others were finished. In fact, if only one of the boys was eating, she wasn't allowed near the plate until he departed. Higgeldy, being a kind lady, imposed no such restrictions on the new arrival. Guilda was welcome any time Higgeldy found herself alone at the dish.

Guilda was frustrated for years, and I can't blame her, now that she is second in seniority among the Friends, for behaving as she does. She forces our younger cats, who have joined us in recent years, to wait until she has dined at leisure before going near the food. She imposes the rule with severe impartiality, and isn't in the least deterred by the fact that one of the youngsters is a husky male almost twice her size. While she eats, he waits, and a single glance is sufficient to send him off to the far side of the kitchen.

In the main, Guilda's presence enlivened the household, and no one, not even Mostly, behaved sluggishly. One day, just as Twink arrived home from school, the pair were playing a spirited game of tag, and when I heard a crash in the kitchen, I hurried out to investigate. Mostly had dashed between Twink's legs, tripping her and causing her to send the kitchen stool-stepladder smashing into the stove.

She sat on the floor, surrounded by her schoolbooks, lunch box, and pencil case. "Mostly," she said tearfully, pointing an accusing finger, "knocked me down. And it's all Guilda's fault!"

VII

THE ART OF REARING A DAUGHTER

Five years after our move to semi-rural Connecticut from New York, my wife and I were divorced. Both of us realized the separation was as necessary as it was painful, and after attempts to reconcile, much hesitation and far too much discussion, we took the step.

I was alone with a daughter just reaching adolescence and, of course, the five Friends.

We lived a little too far from New London for me to hire a full-time maid who would sleep in, and the best I could manage was a cleaning woman who came to the house five days per week. So I assumed a number of new functions, and went to work as best I could. I also refurnished Twink's room, bought her a new wardrobe and advised her, as best I could, in matters that most fathers tend to avoid in their relationships with daughters. In time, and with practice, I became a semi-expert on such subjects as clothes, make-up and boys, among others.

P.J. was quick to become aware of his increased responsibilities, too, and showed no hesitation in meeting them. It was his primary function, as a Best Friend, to give her unstinting love, and this he did in full measure.

When Twink was at home, he spent most of his time with her, far more than he had done previously. In past years, when she had studied, he had stretched out on the floor beside her, much as he had done with me when we had first become Friends. Now, however, he perched on her desk, working his way as close to her schoolbooks as he could, often rubbing his face against the edges of an opened volume that she was reading. When she wrote her reports and essays he rested his chin a fraction of an inch from her paper, his brown nose twitching slightly as it followed the movements of her pen.

Only when she labored on mathematics homework did he decide that loyalty had its limits and turn his back, usually retreating to a far corner of the desk. I refused to believe he actually removed himself when she worked on her algebra, but on several occasions was summoned to her room to witness the phenomenon myself. The only logical explanation I can offer is that Twink, who enjoyed most subjects, shrank from mathematics, and perhaps P.J. sensed her distaste. But there may be those who will accept Twink's claim that he enjoyed literature, found history fascinating, and had a distinct talent for picking up foreign languages, but was hopelessly over his head in the morass of algebra.

When she came downstairs to join me, he came, too; when she returned to her own room, P.J. went with her. When one of her classmates came for a visit, sometimes staying overnight, P.J. was present, sharing in the confidences of girls in their early adolescence. When Twink went from one part of the house to another, he bounded beside her, like a puppy. When she watched television, she had to make room on the chair for him, so he could see the program, too.

I'm relieved to report that he didn't abandon his own aesthetic standards, however. When the cacophonous blare of a rock band filled the music room, P.J. hastily departed and did not return until the television set emitted more soothing sounds. Similarly, he left Twink's room temporarily when rock singers shook the upper reaches of the house on Twink's phonograph. At these critical moments he joined me, and we retreated together toward the farthest sanctuary.

Twink and two of her classmates formed a singing trio and practiced their numbers at the house of one or another of the girls. When it was our turn P.J. and I always steeled ourselves for an ordeal, but Twink and her associates rehearsed only their most dulcet songs under our roof. They were being considerate of P.J., I'm sure, since my pleas for mercy were usually ignored.

Necessity made me the family's Chief Cook, in part because the invention and preparation of dishes long has been a favorite hobby, and I now had the chance to indulge my tastes—at the expense of a daughter too young to protest effectively. In the main Twink liked what I prepared, but on occasion swore I was seeking revenge for being unable to avoid hearing her rock music.

When her homework wasn't too pressing she came to the kitchen to help me prepare dinner. By this time of evening the cats had been fed, and the Friends took themselves elsewhere to sleep off their meal. The Best Friend was always on hand, however, feeling the need and desire to supervise our culinary efforts. It would be unfair to P.J. were I to say he was always underfoot and that we were in constant danger of being tripped as we moved around the kitchen. *Sometimes* he was underfoot, but we were likely to find him on the counter, his nose an inch from a cucumber being sliced, or refusing to budge from the top of the table when the time came for Twink to set it.

We had to use ingenuity to avoid his eager assistance in the preparation of meats. Chicken and even turkey didn't interest him before they were cooked, but swordfish and sea bass impelled him to make a close inspection of what was being seasoned in a broiling pan. He liked steak, too, but chopped sirloin was by all odds his favorite, and he infinitely preferred it to cheaper cuts of ground beef. He liked it well enough when it was served to him raw, and we could sidetrack him for a few minutes by placing some in his dish.

But his need to supervise was overwhelming, and a few tidbits were enough to satisfy him. Then he leaped back onto the counter to watch onion and other seasoning being mixed into the chopped sirloin. I objected on sanitary grounds to the immediate proximity of the Best Friend while preparing food, so P.J. had to be removed from the counter, scolded and told to stay down. He invariably scolded me in return, his manner as irritable as mine, and then appealed to Twink, standing close to her, looking up and meeowing. Only my unyielding firmness prevented her from allowing him to jump back onto the counter.

There were compensations, however, that soothed his ruffled fur. Twink and I always broiled chopped sirloin for three, and P.J. ate from a dish on the floor between her chair and mine. None of the other cats dared to approach him while he was eating from his special dish. Instead, when we were finished, they were given the leftovers in their own dish, and I had to make sure there was enough to take care of all the Friends. My bills for chopped sirloin were enormous.

Although P.J. enjoyed most seafood, he eschewed lobsters, with good cause. One weekend we were expecting a visit from my cousin, Elsa Lichtenstein, the efficient and charming buyer for the huge Barnes and Noble bookstore in New York. Knowing her fondness for lobster, I dashed off to our local waterfront fish market about an hour before her arrival, and returned with a large paper bag literally crawling with live lobsters. Not knowing where to put the bag before boiling the lobsters, I placed it, upright and closed, on the kitchen floor.

The Friends, hearing the lobsters moving around inside the bag, came into the kitchen to investigate. It must have been instinct that impelled them to keep a healthy distance between themselves and the bag. They stood in a semicircle, fascinated, but did not try to make a closer inspection. P.J.'s curiosity, like his courage, was greater than that of the other cats, and he finally moved toward the bag, slowly inching forward, assessing the situation and then taking another step.

When he came within reach he sat, then slapped at the bag repeatedly with a front paw until he toppled it. Again he paused, summoned his nerve and began to worry at the top of the bag. It took him about five minutes to open it. The moment of crisis had arrived, and he no longer hesitated, but boldy advanced into the bag, until all Twink and I could see was his tail.

All at once the tiger-striped gray tail became very bushy. A moment later P.J.'s hind quarters appeared, and little by little the rest of him came into view. He backed out of the bag with great care, as though walking between jagged bits of broken glass. He was escaping from the most horrendous pre-neolithic creatures he had ever seen, and his hair was standing on end.

The Friends, crouching and big-eyed, remained at the far end of the kitchen, watching.

At last P.J. was free of the bag, and his sigh of relief was almost audible as he straightened. He looked at Twink, meeowed silently, having temporarily lost his voice in his fright, and then walked away, his dignity slightly battered but intact.

That night, as Elsa, Twink and I ate lobster, we had company nearby. Yumsie and Mostly hovered a few feet away, waiting for tidbits. So did Higgeldy and Guilda. But P.J. was nowhere to be seen, and after dinner we found him upstairs in Twink's room, enjoying a siesta on her bed. Obviously he had learned that one man's meat is another's poison, and he had no appetite for lobster. Thereafter, whenever we cooked and ate live lobster, P.J. absented himself from the scene. When a dish disagreed with him, he saw no reason to pretend he enjoyed it just because it was an expensive delicacy.

Dr. Harry Brown is the best veterinary surgeon I've ever known. Not only is he proficient, but is endowed with a precious quality, a genuine and abiding affection for the animals he treats. I am inclined to suspect, however, that his patience doesn't extend to humans who make unmitigated nuisances of themselves on the telephone.

P.J. was ill. For several days he had grown increasingly listless, and by the end of the week, when he couldn't make the effort to come downstairs from Twink's room for his breakfast, we knew a visit to his doctor was necessary. I took my car out of the garage, Twink put P.J. into the kitty cage, and off we went. In spite of his condition, P.J. protested vigorously and constantly, yowling at the top of his voice.

He knew something unpleasant was in store, and he crouched, wincing, when he was lifted to Harry Brown's examination table. I couldn't calm him and neither could the doctor; not until Twink soothed and stroked him did he stop trembling.

P.J. required surgery for a urinary ailment commonly found in male cats, and his condition was complicated by an infection that Dr. Brown found it difficult to diagnose. The Best Friend's chances of recovery were dim, Dr. Brown told me privately. Unhappily, Twink heard him.

It is fortunate that she was on vacation from school at the time, as she would have fallen behind in her work. She couldn't read, couldn't listen to her phonograph or watch television. In spite of my repeated urging, she refused to visit any of her friends or invite them to our house. She moped, worried, and became haggard from lack of sleep.

I must admit the days that followed weren't easy for me to endure, either. I needed to exercise to the utmost the qualities of self-discipline that keep any professional author chained to his typewriter in a time of stress. I found I wasn't hungry, either, and concern for P.J. kept me awake nights, too.

Between us, Twink and I must have driven Harry Brown to distraction. We'd have saved money, I think, if we had installed a direct line connecting our house and his veterinary hospital. For a few days the bulletins told us little. P.J. survived the operation, which was successful, but was very weak. Heavy doses of antibiotics were being administered, but time would be needed to determine whether they would be effective in fighting the infection.

On the sixth day of P.J.'s hospitalization he turned the corner and began to improve. On the eleventh day his recovery was assured, and we were asked to fetch him.

P.J. was so weak he could scarcely stand, but he went straight into Twink's arms. There he remained, rumbling like a feeble motorboat on the drive home, while the kitty cage remained unused in the back seat.

"P.J. is an exceptional cat," Harry Brown had told us, confirming what we had known for years. "He's unusually strong, very wiry and has a will of his own. Keep him away from other cats for a few days, as some of them might be inclined to attack him, and he'll recover completely."

Mostly hissed when we walked into the house with P.J., and Yum Yum, the ingrate, followed his example. The odors of the veterinary hospital, we had been told, still clung to P.J., and although we couldn't detect them, they offended the other cats. Guilda bristled, too, and only Higgeldy remained her usual, loving self.

We quickly discovered there was no need for us to protect P.J. Healthy or just beginning a convalescence, he was well able to look after himself. Suddenly, as Twink continued to hold him, he stiffened in her arms and emitted a long, ominous hissing sound.

Yumsie became terrified and fled from the room. Guilda scooted under the nearest sofa, worked her way out the opposite end and silently departed. Higgeldy, who had made no hostile gesture, remained complacent.

Mostly held his ground and growled.

P.J., making an unsuccessful effort to free himself from Twink's grasp, hissed again, and this time the sound was even more menacing.

Mostly wilted and followed Yum Yum to the farthest reaches of the house.

Thereafter the duly warned trio made no attempt to go near the convalescing P.J. Higgeldy joined him on Twink's bed and snuggled there with him, but the others gave him a very wide berth for the next week or two, and he saw to it that they did not impose on him. When the cats were fed, he allowed none but Higgeldy to approach the plate while he ate. The others were forced to wait. In the first days of his recuperation, when he lacked the strength to negotiate the stairs unaided and had to be carried, Higgeldy was the only Friend he allowed to join him on Twink's bed. During this period he lacked the physical prowess to impose his will on the Friends, yet he succeeded in achieving this goal. Even in adversity he remained the Chief Cat.

Our hearts ached when he wobbled precariously trying to walk from one room to another, but his pride remained undiminished. He wanted no help from me, certainly, and growled at me when I tried to carry him. One evening I sat unmoving as, in accordance with his own wishes, he struggled and fought, clawing his way to my lap. Once he reached it he collapsed and rumbled faintly before dropping off to sleep, secure in the knowledge that he had done what he wished in his own way.

Twink put aside all other interests. She gave him his prescribed medication, awakening before dawn so he would take his early morning pill on time. She cooked special, nourishing dishes for him and stayed close beside him while he ate, and she insisted on bringing a kitty litter pan upstairs for his use. In return he gave her his complete love and trust. On several occasions I tried to give him his pill, and I had liked to think that experience had made me adept as an assistant kitty doctor. But P.J. would have none of my ministrations, struggled to escape from me and tried to nip me. Twink, however, was permitted to open his mouth and drop in a pill while he gazed at her adoringly, rumbling.

P.J. paid a return visit to Dr. Brown, was pronounced fit and resumed his normal life. Thereafter he played with Guilda again, sometimes fraternized with Yum Yum and consented to eat with Mostly from the same dish. His energy and physical strength were restored and, on the surface, everything seemed the same as it had been prior to his illness. But when night came he made it evident that something subtle had happened to change his relationships. He allowed Higgeldy to climb onto the foot of Twink's bed, but he forced the other Friends to sleep on the spare bed or leave the room. His devotion to Twink was deeper and more intense than it had ever been, and he had no intention of sharing her with the other Friends.

When Twink began to go on dates with boys I suspected that P.J. would become jealous, but I should have known better. He understood how much she loved him and realized that mere boys offered him no competition. It didn't matter in the least that she went off to parties or that a group of youngsters sometimes filled our living room, music room, and kitchen with laughter and raucous music for an evening.

In spite of Twink's insistence that P.J. thought of himself strictly as people, his generosity didn't extend to the other cats. His illness had made him less patient, and he no longer contented himself with reproachful glances when another of the Friends climbed onto her lap to be stroked. He glared for several minutes, and, if no one took the hint, he approached close enough to drive his rival away. Even Higgeldy was permitted only limited access to his Best Friend.

Boys who were indifferent to cats didn't last long around our house. One, whom Twink liked, made a slighting reference to P.J. on his third or fourth visit. He was sent packing without ado, and was requested not to return. For years Twink sputtered at the mere mention of his name.

As she matured her relationships with boys became less superficial, and eventually she became involved in a romance with a cadet at the United States Coast Guard Academy. Young men are accepted by the Academy only on a competitive basis, and as a result the corps of cadets probably is more intelligent and alert than that enrolled at the other Service academies. Certainly Randy, as I'll call him, because it wasn't his name, was an outstanding example of young American manhood. He was tall and lean, handsome in an off-beat way, and his consistently high grades earned him a regular place on the Dean's List. He was on the list of the Commandant of Cadets for military excellence, too, and was a member of two varsity athletic teams.

Twink was the envy of her friends. Randy escorted her to Academy formals, football games and tea dances. She watched him compete in intercollegiate sports and happily invited him to social events at the girls' school she attended. At least once each weekend, it seemed, Twink and Randy found themselves in our kitchen drinking milk after a party or a movie.

The cat hairs that were everywhere in our house complicated Randy's existence. If he sat in a chair for as long as a minute or two his spotless blue uniform would be covered with the hair that the Friends had shed. Before he returned to his barracks, where he would be subjected to the sharp scrutiny of the upper-class officer-of-the-day, Randy had to be brushed and frequently vacuum-cleaned by Twink.

The young man accepted his fate without complaint, demonstrating a far sunnier disposition than I would have shown. A boy who is enamored of a girl is the most pliably complaisant of all humans, and I was dazed by Twink's manipulation of Randy.

Sometimes, of course, he knew what was happening when she pulled the puppet strings, but, like infatuated youth everywhere and in all ages, he didn't care. Certainly his relationship with P.J. was based on his certain knowledge that if he failed to behave in a sufficiently friendly manner, or if a ring of insincerity entered his praise of the Best Friend, he would be banished forthwith.

Randy, as I have indicated, was no fool. He paid scant attention to the other Friends, but he regularly made the fuss over P.J. that was required of him. Even though his uniform became coated with tiger-striped hair, he put the Best Friend on his lap, stroked him and exclaimed over him.

It was my private opinion, never expressed aloud to Twink, that Randy was going through the motions required of him if he wanted to woo the girl with the inflexible love-me-love-my-Best Friend attitude. Quietly admiring the boy, I could look far into the future and see an admiral's stars gleaming on his shoulder boards.

P.J. realized what Twink was too young and inexperienced to understand, that Randy's loudly proclaimed admiration for him was dictated by sheer necessity. Instead of feeling sorry for the poor boy, P.J. allowed himself to be ruled by the strong feline streak in his nature.

The instant Randy appeared at the door, P.J. paraded back and forth, brushing against him and depositing tiger-striped hair on his trousers. If the cadet was incautious enough to sit down, P.J. completed the job, shedding hair on his tunic or overcoat, or sometimes both. On many occasions I saw the Best Friend put on a finishing touch by leaping onto the back of Randy's chair and mussing his short, carefully brushed hair.

"Put the cat down when he bothers you," I told Randy more than once while he waited for Twink to appear at the beginning of an evening.

Randy always smiled manfully, but there was a hint of pain in his voice when he replied, "I couldn't do that, sir. Noel-Anne might come into the room and see me, sir. And then, sir, what could I possibly say to her?"

P.J. teased Randy unmercifully all through the late winter and early spring. When the warmer weather came, the Academy cadets exchanged their blue uniforms for suntan tropical worsteds and white cottons. Neither of these fabrics picked up cat hair, so Randy was spared. P.J. couldn't be bothered and didn't go near him. But when autumn rolled around and the cadet made his first reappearance in cold weather blues, P.J. swarmed all over him.

In midautumn Twink became interested in another boy, and abruptly stopped dating Randy.

She proved, conclusively, that the adolescent female isn't an unfeeling wretch by allowing her conscience to trouble her for a brief moment one evening. "Daddy," she asked, "do you suppose Randy is badly upset?"

I didn't have the heart to tell her I believed the young man was relieved.

P.J., who sat across the room, grinning, didn't say one word, either.

The sight of luggage invariably upset P.J. I often stay in New York overnight when I'm having meetings with my editors, publishers and agents. I travel, too, for speaking engagements or tours, for necessary research and other business purposes. I also travel for pleasure when I can spare the time, so, for one reason or another, I'm frequently driving somewhere or catching an airplane, train, or ship.

P.J. became disturbed the moment he saw me take suitcases out of the attic. Their appearance meant only one thing: someone he considered a Friend was going away, leaving him behind. His first reaction was an angry one. He meeowed, humping his back, and paced restlessly. Then, his nose very much out of joint because I refused to heed his advice, he disappeared for a time, taking himself elsewhere in the house.

The moment I left an empty or partly packed suitcase unguarded, however, he showed up again, trying more subtle tactics. The most effective of them, he thought, was a brilliantly simple maneuver. He jumped into the suitcase, clawed a nest for himself and curled up there. When I returned and ordered him to move he refused, and if I touched him he growled. His thinking was obvious: if I insisted on going off somewhere, he intended to accompany me.

Failure in his attempts to achieve his goals did not deter him from trying again. Whenever P.J. saw one of my suitcases he made the opportunity to climb into it and resisted removal. When I returned from a trip, however, he didn't bother to go near my luggage. It would serve no useful purpose to bed down in a suitcase, he realized, and fascinating though he found the attic when we didn't want him to dash into it, he had no desire to be locked away there.

Whenever I came home from a trip the Friends gathered to greet me, lining the cellar stairs on the far side of the garage screen that prevented them from climbing all over my car and shredding its paint. P.J., as a rule, was conspicuous by his absence. I wouldn't want to give anyone the idea that he was sulking or carrying a grudge. His subsequent attitude indicated he was intent on proving a point of principle: if I could get along without him, he didn't need me, either. It was his custom to wait for fifteen to thirty minutes, then appear casually while I was unpacking. He would stroll into my bedroom, meeow in an offhand manner, just once, and then head for the door across the room. I had to make amends, of course, so I called to him, stroked him and admired him. Eventually he allowed me to mollify him, and we became Friends again. He bore me no ill will, and proved it by climbing onto my bed and scattering the unpacked contents of the suitcase.

One summer, when I was planning to visit my publishers and literary agents in London and Paris, as well as buckle down to some tricky research for a forthcoming book at the British Museum, I decided Twink was old enough to make her first trip to Europe. She was elated, naturally, but almost immediately became worried about the Friends. We made elaborate arrangements for their care during our absence; our very responsible cleaning woman agreed to feed and look after them, and Pat Fox volunteered to drop in daily to make certain they were in good health and didn't need Harry Brown's services.

Twink had gone off on a number of short trips, the longest of them a ten-day jaunt to Washington, D.C. But this trip was different, and when P.J. saw the luggage accumulating in her room he went wild. He scolded her incessantly, following her around the house and talking without a pause. He tried, in vain, to destroy her luggage, ripping only one old case that needed replacement.

When she opened the luggage he made a real nuisance of himself, climbing into one case, then another, and it took her far longer to pack than would have been the case had he cooperated. I suggested that she shut him out of her room until she finished packing, but she couldn't and wouldn't subject him to such cruel treatment.

P.J. went into hiding shortly before we left, and we almost missed our train to New York because Twink refused to leave until she found him and said goodbye to him. I located them at the back of the house, where they were snuggling and rumbling like motorboats, and had to drag Twink away.

The trip was an unqualified success. Twink went sightseeing, exercised her excellent command of French in Paris, fell in love with the Egyptian collection in the British Museum and managed to gain no weight, although she ate and ate. She met some groovy boys on board ship eastward bound, and still more on the westward voyage. She returned home with a new wardrobe, broadened horizons and a number of catnip toys and other gifts for the Friends.

When we arrived home I unlocked the door and started to bring in our baggage, Twink several paces behind me with some of the lighter pieces. Yum Yum, always the first to greet a returning traveler, was standing at the door, ready to shed black and white hair on my trousers. Mostly hauled himself down from his sofa seat and headed toward the door. Guilda clawed the molding, and Higgeldy started to play with a luggage tag.

I caught a glimpse of P.J., who apparently had been in the kitchen, but who headed elsewhere the moment I unlocked and opened the door. I called to him, but he ignored me and headed toward the rear of the house. Confident that we would follow our usual routine, I made no attempt to pursue him.

When Twink walked in, the four Friends immediately surrounded her, each clamoring. She dropped to her knees in order to give them the attention they deserved and required, and everyone was very happy. She, too, had been subjected to P.J.'s absent treatment in the past, and wasn't disturbed.

The Best Friend, however, could not keep himself

away. He hadn't seen Twink in six weeks, and her presence, the sound of her voice, her laughter were more than he could bear. We heard a scampering sound emanating from the interior of the house, and then P.J. appeared, running as fast as he could, his ears plastered against his head, his tail outstretched.

He leaped over several pieces of luggage, clearing them with ease, and literally threw himself into Twink's arms. She wept as she hugged him, and he clung to her, burying his wet, brown nose in her neck. It was a glorious reunion, and for days thereafter the Best Friends were inseparable.

VIII

THE WOMAN WHO HATED CATS

Marilyn is a woman of high principle and equally high standards. An anesthetist by profession, she was esteemed by her colleagues, respected by the surgeons with whom she worked and admired by her patients. I find intelligence, principle, and beauty an irresistible as well as a dazzling combination, and inasmuch as she is the loveliest woman I have ever known, it was impossible for me to avoid falling in love with her. When inspired I tend to become persuasive, so she agreed to marry me.

Our future, we knew, would not be free of problems. She would assume a delicate maternal relationship with a girl in her teens. I would become the father of three small children, one of whom, Michele, was troubled by some of her early memories. In addition, Marilyn confessed one day, "I hate cats." Obviously we had our work cut out for us.

I was apprehensive the night I broke the big news to Twink, but she accepted my revelation with monumental calm. "I think it's cool," she said, "really neat. I've been wondering for months how long it would take you to get up enough nerve to propose."

The smaller children were equally serene. Margot, we discovered, was busily telling all her friends of preschool age that she had instructed us to marry, and that we were wisely following her advice.

Relations between Marilyn and the Friends, however, remained cool. P.J. sauntered over whenever Marilyn visited the house, said a few words and then wandered away again. He was making no premature judgments, and the others, it seemed, were waiting to take their cue from the Chief Cat.

The surface situation indicated cause for concern, but I believed I had private cause for optimism because I could not accept Marilyn's alleged dislike of cats as valid. The reason was simple: she already had a cat of her own, Inky, a coal-black female with a friendly disposition. It seemed unlikely that a cat-hater would be a cat-owner, but I kept my thoughts to myself.

Marilyn decided to leave Inky with her parents, with whom she, the children and Inky had been living, rather than move a full-grown animal into a house already overflowing with full-grown animals. She had other reasons, too. "My father," she said, "claims he can't stand Inky, but he's secretly very fond of her. And with all of us leaving, I don't want him to become too lonely."

She didn't sound like a woman who despised cats, but I continued to keep my mouth shut.

Builders arrived to add several new rooms to our house, and preparations moved into high gear.

"I won't permit those cats to jump up onto the kitchen counters," Marilyn said. "It isn't sanitary."

She was right, of course, and I certainly couldn't blame someone who had been a registered nurse and then an anesthetist from being sensitive in such matters. "I've tried," I told her, "and have always found it easier in the long run to wipe off the counters with an antiseptic solution. But good luck, and more power to you."

The day of the wedding came, and we defied tradition by driving together, with all of us in one car. After all, we were going to be a family, and should be united from the outset. When we had settled ourselves in the car I felt impelled to make a brief speech; the occasion, I thought, called for appropriate remarks.

"Children," I began, "now that Mummy and Daddy are going to get married—"

I was interrupted by Twink's suppressed whoop of gleeful laughter.

Whatever I had intended to say went out of my mind. We were off to a flying start.

Hoping to give Twink and Michele a greater sense of family unity, Marilyn and I had decided to take them with us on a brief "honeymoon" trip. As we have since explained to incredulous friends, it seemed like a good idea. Well, the girls had a wonderful time.

On our return the whole family settled into the house,

and in the months that followed, most of our problems resolved themselves. Marilyn and Twink hit it off from the start, and soon founded a relationship that was intimate as well as solid. Twink had not only found a confidante whom she respected, but willingly accepted Marilyn's authority. I was no longer forced to flounder in the unfamiliar world of giving feminine guidance to a teen-aged daughter, and I felt a deep sense of gratification as I saw Marilyn and Twink establish a rapport.

Margot and Paul, who were little more than babies, accepted me without qualification as Daddy. We played together, enjoyed adventures together, and they learned new disciplines. Daddy's study was off-limits, and they didn't play noisy games within earshot of it. There were all sorts of new rules, all sorts of new games, too, and life was exciting.

Michele, who was a trifle older, required more careful handling. She and I sat down for a long, private chat every day, and she accompanied me on my rounds of "Saturday errands." Within a far shorter time than Marilyn and I had allowed ourselves to hope, Michele and I achieved a mutual understanding that has continued to expand and grow deeper through the years.

A pair of anxious parents had anticipated difficulties between Twink and the smaller children, but we had been seeing ghosts. Twink, too long an only child, was delighted to have two little sisters and a very little brother, and there was sufficient difference in their ages that she felt no sense of sibling-rivalry. The little people worshiped Twink, who could do no wrong in their eyes, and Michele gave her a new title: Assistant Mummy.

The children and the Friends formed a close association from the outset, too. Thanks to Inky, the youngsters felt at home with cats, and the Friends were equally at ease. Yum Yum, Higgeldy, and Guilda enjoyed their romps with Margot and Paul. Mostly, somewhat more reserved, played with them, too, and began sleeping on Paul's bed, while Higgeldy, when she wasn't in Twink's room, napped on Margie's bed. Michele urgently requested and was granted the right to help feed the Friends and clean the kitty litter, tasks she has since assumed herself. Trying to emulate the teen-ager, she soon sat with one or more cats on her lap.

P.J. saw to it that his own relationship with the children was unique. They quickly observed his special dignity, and, realizing he was the Chief Cat, treated him accordingly. He, always gentle with children, enjoyed a frolic with them, but quickly took himself elsewhere if their exuberance threatened rough treatment.

"If I pulled P.J.'s tail," Paul said, soon after moving in, "he would bite me."

"If you pull P.J.'s tail," an indignant Margot told him, "*I'll* bite you."

P.J., recognizing the difference between the intentions of small children and their ability to fulfill them, did not tempt fate. Unlike the younger cats, he did not climb onto the lap of a child for a session of motorboat rumbling and stroking. He did not object, however, when a child sat down on a sofa beside him, and made no attempt to move away when patted. He no longer deigned to chase toys pulled along the floor by a string, and for weeks ignored attempts by the children to tempt him into playing such games.

Margot was upset by what appeared to be his indifference, and P.J., being tender-hearted, was disturbed by her inability to understand his feelings. There was only one way to handle the situation, so he began to chase after kitty toys she pulled around the house for his benefit. When Michele and Paul tried to follow Margot's example, however, P.J. refused to budge. He knew they were merely being imitative, and that their hearts weren't really in the game.

The question of Marilyn's relationship with the Friends remained unresolved. She waged unrelenting war on any cat who climbed up onto the kitchen counters, a struggle that continues down to the present day, and she enjoyed a limited success. When a Friend who happened to jump on a counter saw her coming, he or she promptly went elsewhere, waited until she left the kitchen and then returned. The cats continue to follow this farsighted, wise policy.

P.J., of course, refused to dissemble. Marilyn soon discovered she could not shoo him off, and had to lift him down.

"*Enh, enh,*" he told her when she put him on the floor for the sixth or tenth time in a single day, and although he was too much of a gentleman to laugh at her, there was a gleam of humor in his eyes.

Having taken a strong stand, Marilyn tried hard to maintain it. "I don't feed the cats or take care of them in any way," she told me repeatedly. "I hate cats."

As every husband knows, a man doesn't argue with his wife when it is impossible for him to win a debate. One evening, however, Guilda happened to be curled up on Marilyn's lap, and the lady of the house was stroking the Friend as she made her usual speech.

I had the temerity to observe that there was a seeming discrepancy between her words and deeds.

"Not at all," she replied with pure feminine logic. "Guilda is very pretty and cute, and I'm not a mean person, so I'm hardly going to throw her off my lap when she's rumbling like a motorboat. But that doesn't mean I like her."

I found discretion the better part of valor and made no comment when Marilyn allowed Yum Yum and, now and again, Higgeldy, to join us on our bed at night. I'm sure she would have told me that Friends, like people, need beds if they want to enjoy a good night's sleep.

By exerting considerable ingenuity, Marilyn was able to maintain the façade of her attitude. When Mostly stretched out a few feet from her chair, his green eyes fixed on her adoringly, she could point to him and say, "Look at him! He's positively glaring at me. Now I hope you can understand why I hate cats. They hate me!"

P.J. gave no indication that he either accepted or rejected Marilyn's proclaimed attitude. He came to her every evening, while she was reading or sewing, and requested recognition. A lady needs cause to snub someone she knows, so Marilyn patted him before she returned to other activities. P.J., too proud to press the matter, invariably left her for the lap of someone who would give him the undivided attention he knew he deserved.

The problem reached the crisis stage on the day that Paul started nursery school. The girls were off at their own schools, so Marilyn and I were alone at lunch. Then P.J. decided to join us, and sat down beside me, meeowing politely as he asked for his usual mealtime tidbits.

I happened to be eating a cold roast beef sandwich, and gave him a small piece of meat.

"I object to the feeding of cats when we're eating," Marilyn said.

"P.J. has been coming around this way for many years, and I can't change the habits of his lifetime," I replied. "What's more, I wouldn't—even if I could."

She glared, challenging me.

I returned the glare, accepted the challenge and gave P.J. another bit of meat.

Marital ties were somewhat strained for the rest of the day.

Marilyn, being a sensible woman, didn't mention the subject again. I, being somewhat less sensible, continued to give P.J. table tidbits, but fed him more or less surreptitiously. We had reached a real impasse.

About a month after the incident at the lunch table, Marilyn announced, as she sat down in the living room after returning home from church, that she was chilly.

I happened to think the room was warm, and had already shed my jacket; glancing at her, I saw she was wearing a heavy sweater over a high-necked, long-sleeved wool dress. "Aren't you feeling well?" I asked.

"Oh, I'm fine," she assured me.

It occurred to me that her face looked flushed. "Do you have a fever?"

She laughed with the superiority of one in the medical profession.

I went off to our bathroom for the thermometer.

"I don't need to have my temperature taken," Marilyn said indignantly when I returned.

"Prove it to me," I said, launching into a long harangue.

Hoping to silence me, she took the thermometer and popped it into her mouth.

She had a temperature of 105 degrees.

I immediately telephoned our physician, who told me to bring her to the hospital, saying he would meet us there.

Marilyn protested bitterly all the way to the hospital, insisting she wasn't ill.

After the examination, complete with X rays, Dr. Richard Barry told me, as he telephoned the admitting office to request a private room, that she had a severe case of pneumonia and would require hospitalization.

"You tell her, Dick," I said. "She insists she's going home right now."

Marilyn spent the next two weeks under treatment at the hospital.

When she was finally allowed to go home she was instructed to go straight to bed and stay there. She did—for seven weeks, and her slow, difficult convalescence may have convinced her she doesn't have the stamina and strength of a peasant, as she had always tried to believe.

Twink, the Assistant Mummy, took over additional duties during those seven weeks. Michele, always a helpful little girl, worked hard. I took on some additional chores myself. All of the children were exceptionally well-behaved, and visited Mummy for short periods so they wouldn't tire her.

The Friends were thoughtful, too, and held their visits to a minimum.

P.J., however, felt the time had come for him to take charge. Marilyn, he decided, needed someone to look after her, make certain she took her medicines on schedule and, above all, keep her company. Whether she knew it or not, he thought, she was lonely; *he* knew, and he acted accordingly.

For seven uninterrupted weeks P.J. spent his days and nights on Marilyn's bed, leaving her side only to eat a quick meal or relieve himself. Anyone unacquainted with P.J. might have found it difficult to believe that any animal could demonstrate such unswerving devotion. P.J. himself didn't see the situation in that light. Not only was he doing his duty, but he *wanted* to spend every moment with Marilyn.

For the first time in his life, not even "nicies," as we had called them for years, could tempt him. There were two kinds of nicies. One consisted of the tidbits he was fed at the table. The other was the dry cat food, placed in a separate dish, that the Friends ate as snacks.

P.J. long had numbered among his positions that of managing director of the nicies dish. When it was empty he trotted up to us, meeowing, starting toward the kitchen and then coming back to meeow again.

"What do you want?" we asked him. "Show me!"

He did, trotting out to the dish in the kitchen and talking at a lightning pace.

During Marilyn's illness he neglected his duties at the nicies dish. If the Friends emptied it, there were no replacements until Twink, Michele, or I became aware of the situation and remedied it.

Snacks had been important to P.J., but now they literally didn't matter. Even when informed that the nicies dish was empty and was about to be refilled, he wouldn't leave Marilyn's bed. We tried rattling the cardboard box of dry cat food, always a sure-fire way to summon even the Best Friend, but he looked up for an instant, his ears perking, and then burrowed closer to his patient.

Literally nothing induced him to abandon her.

When Marilyn first came home from the hospital she was still too ill and weak to pay more than token attention to P.J.'s fidelity. Thereafter, I noticed, she was usually stroking him with one hand while holding a book in the other. No matter how deeply she might be engrossed in her reading, she was returning P.J.'s affection.

I took care not to discuss the changed relationship with her. I had no way of knowing how either of them might feel once she was completely recovered. And, strictly speaking, their regard or lack of it was their business, not mine.

After what seemed like an interminable period of waiting, Marilyn finally left her bed. We celebrated by having lunch together, alone, as all the children were at school, and I took time off from work to broil a steak.

P.J. quietly accompanied Marilyn to the table.

Her appetite had returned, and she enjoyed her onion soup. She ate a bite or two of steak, then cut a slice into smaller pieces. Silently, without fanfare, she began to give tidbits to P.J.

His joy was so great he discarded the fundamentals of discretion, and meeowing insistently, called my attention to the altered situation.

I raised an eyebrow.

A man apologizes or finds rationalizations when he makes changes in fundamental principle, but a woman accepts such a reversal as normal, natural and, I dare say, inevitable. "P.J. is hungry, so I'm giving him some nicies,"

Marilyn said calmly. She fed him again, and dismissed the subject with a shrug.

Practice makes perfect only when the practitioner is endowed with natural or acquired skills. For years I've daubed flea powder on cats, given them pills and treated them for ear mites. And for all those years the Friends have known from bitter experience that I'm a bumbling amateur.

Yum Yum has fled when he's heard me take a pill bottle from a drawer in a kitchen cabinet. Higgeldy has demonstrated astonishing strength in her attempts to escape from me when I, equally determined, have tried to drop a pill down her throat. Mostly, ostrich-like, has hidden his head in a corner when he's seen me pick up a can of flea powder. And Guilda has become terror-stricken when she's seen me approach, carrying an ear-dropper.

Only P.J., feeling sorry for me, has steeled himself and made no protest when I've given him medication. In the years when no one else was available to help him, he knew he had no choice.

None of the Friends has suffered traumas when Twink has ministered to them. Her love for them was so intense that, when she first shook a pill into her palm and approached P.J. with it, she knew what to do and how to do it. The Friends, to my dismay, have never fled at *her* approach, and actually have welcomed her efforts.

Michele received her initial training as a kitty doctor at the age of eight. By the time she was nine she could give a Friend his or her pills unaided. Only the intricacies of giving a complicated ear mite treatment eluded her by the time she reached her tenth birthday. At eleven

146

she was self-confident and sure-handed. Some people have it, obviously, and some of us don't.

Marilyn, as a self-styled cat-hater, gave the cats no pills, no treatments. When I struggled alone, against odds, I nevertheless refrained from asking for her help. After all, she administered anesthesia to humans, so it would have been presumptuous of me.

She made no change in this policy after her recovery from the long bout of pneumonia. She had established a new, intimate relationship with P.J., it was true, but just because she loved him didn't mean she liked cats.

That summer an epidemic of ear mites made life miserable for the Friends. The cure is long, dreary, and difficult, so the humans were unhappy, too. The patient is wrapped in a large towel so he can't claw his benefactors, and is held by one person. Then the chief kitty doctor inserts drops in the cat's ears, cleans out the canals and inserts more drops. This treatment, when administered twice weekly for several months to five cats, is a chore.

One hot night Twink and I were in the cellar, treating the Friends. The girls went into hiding and had to be found. The boys fought manfully. Higgeldy and Guilda wept and complained when I, the assistant, wrapped and held them. Yum Yum and Mostly saw nothing to be gained by enduring torture in silence, and howled.

Then it was P.J.'s turn, and I started toward the cellar stairs to find him.

At that moment Marilyn came down the stairs, carrying him. He was at peace in her arms, and, although he probably knew what was coming, made no attempt to escape.

Marilyn brushed past me as though I weren't there.

"Why don't I help you?" she asked Twink casually, not bothering to mention the obvious, my incompetence.

"That," Twink said fervently, "would be groovy!"

Thereafter I was excluded. I gave the Friends no pills, aided in no ear mite or other treatments. The cats brightened and lived happier, richer—not to mention healthier —lives. Twink breathed more easily, and her tasks became simpler.

Marilyn said nothing about her new status, at least to me. She and Twink took it for granted. There were two kitty doctors in the house now, both of them skilled and gentle. Eventually, when Twink went off to college, there was one.

When a cat balks and decides to spit up a pill, it becomes a nightmare to force the animal to swallow the capsule. I've known Higgeldy to get rid of a pill eight or ten times before escaping from me without medication. So I've secretly watched Marilyn, hoping to learn from her technique, but I don't know how she does it.

Using two fingers as persuaders, she opens a cat's mouth. Just like that, swiftly, without force. Simultaneously, in what to me is miraculous coordination, she drops in the pill with her other hand. It stays in, and the cat swallows. Higgeldy, who causes me such problems, calmly wanders to the milk bowl for a drink. Marilyn washes her hands, no longer bothering to bestow a pitying smile on me.

Her technique in administering an ear mite treatment is still more impressive. She doesn't bother to wrap the patient in a towel, and requires the help of no assistant. In five minutes she can complete a task, efficiently and neatly, that took me more than a half-hour to accomplish badly. I won't say the Friends look forward to her treatments, but they don't struggle, and offer no more than token protests. They know she's treating them for their own good, and they submit with a minimum of fuss.

They don't howl, claw or fight. When she's finished they don't race out of the room and sulk for the rest of the evening. They stay near her and within a few moments are either rubbing against her leg or jumping into her lap, where they know they'll be petted and soothed.

One evening a friend Marilyn and I had known separately, prior to our marriage, dropped in for a visit. Complications in her own life had occupied her, and we hadn't seen her in years.

"You know," she said after watching a parade of children and animals through the living room, "you two have courage. With four children and five cats, you're outnumbered."

We shrugged, and I lied baldly, saying it was no trick at all.

Marilyn, who is an honest woman, demurred. Most of the time, she said, we were ringmasters in a circus. She was interrupted by P.J., who climbed into her lap, Higgeldy, who rubbed against her leg, and Guilda, who perched on the arm of her chair, almost upsetting her drink.

The visitor commented on the obvious esteem in which the Friends held her.

"Well," Marilyn said, "I sometimes think I missed my calling and should have been a vet."

"I don't doubt your ability to handle them," the visitor

said. "But why should *they* trust *you*—as they obviously do?"

"Cats are like children," Marilyn said with a pleased smile. "They know, instinctively, when someone loves them."

IX

All, soon or late, are doom'd
  That path to tread.—HOMER

An open trunk stood in the middle of Twink's room, and
near it was a foot locker already crammed with linens,
blankets and a variety of odds and ends. Suitcases were
piled on the chairs and spare bed, and there were
clothes everywhere, dresses and coats, skirts and blouses
and sweaters and shoes. The chaos was beyond description.

P.J. surveyed the scene with resignation if not equanimity. Twink had held several long talks with him, and
assured me he understood that when a young woman
went off to college, it wasn't the same as taking a trip.

I believe he really did know that the time had come for her to acquire a higher education and that she wasn't going off on a frivolous pleasure-seeking jaunt.

He offered no complaints, verbal or physical, and didn't try to burrow into any of her luggage. Instead he found himself a small, clear space on the top of her dresser, and from that vantage point he watched everything she did. He was sober, dignified and unusually silent.

The other Friends, being mere cats, had no idea what was happening, and amused themselves by playing hide-and-seek in the luggage. It was best for them, Twink said, as it would help no one if they became upset.

The day Marilyn and I drove Twink off to college P.J. indulged in none of his pre-journey antics. He refused to let her out of his sight, and after they exchanged private farewells in her room he accompanied her to the cellar, then stood on the stairs with his brown nose pushed through an opening in the garage screen as he watched her climb into the car and drive away.

Twink wept, her concern over their parting so intense she found it difficult to anticipate the excitements and challenges of the new life that lay ahead.

She was a faithful correspondent that year, and every letter contained the same message. *Give the Friends my love*, she wrote, *especially P.J.*

We spoke on the telephone at least twice weekly, and Twink soon acquired the habit of calling every Sunday, promptly at noon. "How are the Friends?" was her greeting. "How is P.J., my Best Friend?"

I saw to it that P.J. was nearby as noon approached on Sundays, and frequently Twink spoke to him. I held the receiver near his ear, and he perked up when he heard and recognized her voice. Sometimes emotion overcame him, rendering him speechless, but often he replied with a happy meeow, then told her he was well and that he missed her. Occasionally he rumbled like a motorboat.

Twink was ecstatic whenever she heard his voice on the telephone.

The reunions of the Best Friends were almost painful in their joyous intensity. They hugged, snuggled and were inseparable every moment Twink spent in the house; at night P.J. offered no apologies when he deserted Marilyn and me to sleep on Twink's bed. Other old habits remained unchanged, too. Sometimes Twink brought work home with her over a weekend or vacation, and P.J., curling up on her desk, studied with her. He enjoyed reading Voltaire in the original, Twink reported, and shared her passion for anthropology.

Not once did he absent himself or otherwise indicate a sense of hurt when she came home, not once did he sulk when she went back to college. He, like the rest of us, Twink included, accepted her new way of life and became acclimated to it.

The other Friends were delighted to see her when she came home, too, and she gave all of them her unstinting love. She was never alone, and the instant she walked into the house frolicking Friends and shouting little children surrounded her.

I might add that, to this day, the children believe Twink can do no wrong. When she and Jim come for a visit, Michele drags her off and tells her secrets too important to be entrusted to a mere mother and father. This past summer Margot's letters from camp faithfully informed us she was having fun and requested us to give Twink her love. She rarely said anything else in them, and, we later discovered, also corresponded with Twink, too. Recently, when Paul fell off a swing on which he was performing acrobatics, and broke his arm, his first demand was that we tell Twink the portentous news.

I had tried, before Twink went off to college, to prepare her for the possibility that something might happen to one or more of the Friends while she was away. Both of us found the subject too painful to discuss in detail.

A crisis erupted very suddenly, about three months after Twink went off to school. Yum Yum, who had appeared in good health on Friday evening, was very ill on Saturday morning, and I rushed him off to see Dr. Brown. He was gravely ill, sinking fast and was beyond hope of recovery. Yumsie, always gentle until this critical moment, was in such anguish that he bit me, opening a wound that required stitches.

Dr. Brown suggested he be put away so his suffering wouldn't be prolonged.

I took a deep breath and agreed.

The doctor's assistant hadn't yet arrived for work, and Harry Brown asked me to hold Yumsie while he was given an injection. I could have refused, but my weakness would have condemned Yumsie to undergo additional agony.

He looked up at me, his expression one of complete trust, and then closed his eyes. I stood frozen as Harry Brown carried him out of the operating room, blood-flecked froth covering his mouth.

I've lived through that scene again, more often than I can recall, and will never forget it.

After my own injury had been attended at the emergency room of the hospital, I returned home and telephoned Twink at college. All I told her was that I wanted to drive up and take her to dinner, but she had a date that night.

"Tomorrow night, then," I said.

"Okay." An anxious note crept into her voice. "What's wrong, Daddy?"

I struggled at length before I could speak the one word, "Yumsie."

Twink was silent at the other end of the line.

The following evening, after picking her up at school, I took her to dinner. It was a miserable experience for both of us. Twink's eyes were red-rimmed, and we exchanged only a few words. I refrained from telling her any details, and she asked few questions. One thought, I knew, was present in Twink's mind as well as mine. We realized that an era was coming to an end, and, beyond our grief for Yumsie, we were thinking of P.J.

Six months later we lost Mostly. He developed an ailment of the urinary tract, and medication did not alleviate the condition, so surgery was required. Ordinarily such an operation is simple and isn't regarded as major, so I wasn't particularly concerned when I left Mostly at the vet's. All of our male cats had undergone similar surgery at one time or another, and I expected to return for him in a day or two.

Several hours later Harry Brown called me to say that Mostly had expired in his sleep, under anesthesia, on the operating table. His overweight condition had done irreparable damage to his heart.

Twink, when I telephoned her the news, sounded resigned and very weary. She was maturing, growing rapidly to womanhood.

Now the ranks of the Friends were reduced to three. Higgeldy and Guilda spent several days searching the house for Mostly, and even P.J. joined in the hunt for his one-time enemy.

"It feels strange," Twink said when she came home on her next vacation, and stood, hugging P.J. "The house is so empty."

We looked at each other for an instant, then glanced at P.J., and Twink quickly turned away.

The remaining Friends soon adjusted to their new situation. P.J. continued to romp with the girls, playing tag and race horse. On warm summer evenings they sat inside screened windows, watching the night creatures. One day P.J. managed to worm his way into the attic, retreated to the dark, far reaches and, behaving like a naughty kitten, refused to come out. We had to leave him there for an hour before he could be persuaded to change his mind.

There was ample room for the remaining Friends at the cat food dish now, but Guilda was still required to wait until P.J. and Higgeldy finished a meal before she was allowed to approach it. Old habits are hard to break, and she didn't seem to mind.

The next year passed swiftly. P.J. enjoyed vigorous good health and developed none of the infirmities of old age. Because of his advanced years we took him to Harry Brown for a checkup, and, as always, he protested loudly, hating the kitty cage. On the homeward drive he reproved me at length for subjecting him to what he considered a totally unnecessary indignity.

In Twink's sophomore year, on a Thursday in mid-march, I was surprised when Twink telephoned us one morning. Her voice was a shade too calm as she said, "I'm coming home Saturday after my eleven o'clock class. I have all kinds of things I've got to do here on Sunday, so I can just stay for twenty-four hours."

I told her we'd be delighted, then asked, "Is there any special reason you're coming?"

"I just want to come home for a day, that's all," she said evasively.

I was somewhat puzzled, as she hadn't made it a practice to leave school for no reason, and although I didn't want to pry, I asked, "Have a fight with Jim?"

"Oh, no!" She sounded as though the very idea shocked her.

The mystery was deepening. "Look," I said, "don't get the idea that I'm trying to discourage you. But, if I remember correctly, your mid-term exams start this coming Monday."

"They do," she said. "I'm planning to study on the train, and I'm bringing tons of books with me."

Her projected trip made no sense, and I said so.

"I'm coming," Twink said, her voice thickening, "because I want to see P.J."

I can't explain the phenomenon of her premonition or the intensity of her foreboding, and can only report facts, accurately.

That evening P.J. wasn't particularly hungry, and only picked at his food. On Friday morning I heard a crash in the kitchen, then P.J. howled in brief but deep protest. I found him squatting near the overturned nicies dish, and dry cat food was scattered everywhere. As nearly as I could determine, he had jumped from the top of the refrigerator to the dish, as he had done so many hundreds of times in the past, and somehow had lost his footing.

In a few moments he seemed completely recovered, and his nose was cold and wet, so we decided not to take him to the vet, but to watch him.

When Twink arrived home early Saturday afternoon, P.J. was listless. She was not in the least surprised by his condition.

She took him off to her room while she studied; he spent the afternoon on her desk, his nose a fraction of an inch from an opened book, and that evening he curled up on her lap when she moved to an easy chair in her room. We saw her only at dinner, and, briefly, at lunch the next day.

Before Twink returned to school she brought P.J. down to the living room and put him on a couch. Then, for an hour before she departed, she stroked him, her face close to his, and spoke to him in a low murmur that no one else could hear. Occasionally he answered with a soft or silent meeow.

At one point I glanced at them for an instant, and a lump formed in my throat. I had to leave the room.

On Monday morning P.J. was so lethargic he didn't respond to the kitty call when I summoned the Friends to breakfast. I carried him to the kitchen, and he sat a few paces from the kitty dish. Guilda was hungry, and he watched her, making no protest when she ate.

Marilyn volunteered to take him to the vet, and I nodded.

P.J. was curled up on our bed, where Marilyn had placed him, and appeared to be asleep. I stroked him, and he opened his eyes long enough to look at me. I went straight to my study.

An hour later Marilyn joined me there. P.J.'s collapse had been swift, and he was suffering from several ailments, each of them serious: feline anemia, severe lung congestion and a critical kidney infection. Until that morning his temperature had been normal, but now he was running a very high fever, too.

There was literally no chance he could recover, and Dr. Brown advised that he be put away, but Marilyn had asked him to wait until I gave my approval.

"Tell him," I said, "not to hurt P.J."

Marilyn went up to the house to make the call, and I sat numbly at my desk until I heard from Harry Brown.

Then I put in a call for Twink, who was taking her first exam.

An hour or so later I heard her voice.

"Hi, Twink," I said, and lost my voice.

There was a prolonged silence, and at last she said, "I know."

Melanie, also known as Menalie and Charlie Girl, was very small when Marilyn brought her home. She was a sweet, loving kitten, and Twink's heart went out to her when they first met. We knew how much she missed the Friends in her new home, and she reverted to childhood for an instant, her expression beatific, when we suggested that she and Jim might want to take Melanie home with them.

Georgy-Porgy—his full name is St. George Henry St. Paul—is a very active, mischievous young fellow who keeps Higgeldy and Guilda active in their maturity. He is tan and white, and came to the door one day, as a kitten, when Marilyn was calling Paul home for dinner.

Georgy, in the opinion of Harry Brown's assistant, is the friendliest cat she has ever seen, and I'm inclined to agree. He finds laps irresistible, he rumbles like a motorboat the instant we speak to him, and he squinges expertly.

I sometimes think the main purpose of Twink's visits to us is to see Higgeldy, Guilda, and Georgy. Even Jim, who claims he doesn't care much for cats—Melanie, for whom he buys kitty candy, excepted—would be tempted to drive away with Georgy if his father-in-law didn't keep a sharp watch.

Recently, when Twink was stroking Georgy and he was squinging at her, she said, "In some ways Georgy is very much like P.J." Her tone changed. "But in others, he isn't. Nobody is."

She's right: there was only one P.J. I often dream of him, and so does Twink.